MORE OCAML *Algorithms, Methods & Diversio*

In *More OCaml* John Whitington takes a meandering tour of functional programming with OCaml, introducing various language features and describing some classic algorithms. The book ends with a large worked example dealing with the production of PDF files. There are questions for each chapter together with worked answers and hints.

More OCaml will appeal both to existing OCaml programmers who wish to brush up their skills, and to experienced programmers eager to explore functional languages such as OCaml. It is hoped that each reader will find something new, or see an old thing in a new light. For the more casual reader, or those who are used to a different functional language, a summary of basic OCaml is provided at the front of the book.

JOHN WHITINGTON founded a software company which uses OCaml extensively. He teaches functional programming to students of Computer Science at the University of Cambridge. His other books include *"PDF Explained"* (O'Reilly, 2012) and *"OCaml from the Very Beginning"* (Coherent, 2013).

MORE OCAML

Algorithms, Methods & Diversions

John Whitington

COHERENT PRESS

COHERENT PRESS
Cambridge

Published in the United Kingdom by Coherent Press, Cambridge

© Coherent Press 2014

This publication is in copyright. Subject to statutory
exception no reproduction of any part may take place
without the written permission of Coherent Press.

First published August 2014
Reprinted with corrections July 2015
Reprinted 2016
Updated for OCaml language changes October 2017

A catalogue record for this book is available from the British Library

ISBN 978-0-9576711-1-9 Paperback

by the same author

PDF Explained (O'Reilly, 2012)
OCaml from the Very Beginning (Coherent, 2013)
A Machine Made this Book: Ten Sketches of Computer Science (Coherent, 2016)

Contents

Summary of Basic OCaml	ix
Our Working Environment	xiii
1 Unravelling "Fold"	1
2 Being Lazy	9
3 Named Tuples with Records	15
4 Generalized Input/Output	21
5 Streams of Bits	27
6 Compressing Data	35
7 Labelled and Optional Arguments	51
8 Formatted Printing	57
9 Searching for Things	63
10 Finding Permutations	71
11 Making Sets	79
12 Playing Games	93
GENERATING PDF DOCUMENTS - AN EXTENDED EXAMPLE	98
13 Representing Documents	101
14 Writing Documents	107
15 Pretty Pictures	117
16 Adding Text	123
Answers to Questions	131
Hints for Questions	189
Coping with Errors	195
Index	201

Preface

When I wrote "OCaml from the Very Beginning", the intention was to have a book with no prerequisites – a bright individual, new to programming, could follow it. Because of this, and for length concerns, plenty of interesting material had to be omitted. This text, not being constrained in the same way, contains a variety of topics which require some existing experience with a functional language. Those who have read the previous text should have no problem with this one. Equally, it should be comprehensible to a functional programmer familiar with another language such as Standard ML or Haskell. The reader may need to make occasional reference to the OCaml manual.

There are, typically, two different activities when writing programs larger than a few dozen lines: firstly, dealing with the challenges of complexity inherent in the problem, by finding appropriate abstraction mechanisms and, secondly, finding and using the wide range of third-party libraries available for a given language. Most projects involve a combination of the two. In this text we concentrate wholly on the former, using nothing other than the OCaml Standard Library. Keeping up with the myriad third-party OCaml libraries is a task better suited to other media.

The book consists of sixteen short chapters falling broadly into three categories. Some introduce pieces of OCaml syntax with worked examples. Some survey practical topics such as input/output. Some cover little diversions or puzzles. The main matter of the book ends with a lengthy worked example: a program to build PDF files containing computer-generated drawings and text. There are full answers and hints for all questions in the book, and additional material in the online resources.

Acknowledgments

The quotation in Chapter 6 is taken from ISO-32000 © International Organization for Standardization. The tables of codes in the same chapter are taken from ITU-T T.30 © International Telecommunication Union. The presentation of the balancing operation for Red-Black trees in Chapter 11 and its functional implementation is due to Chris Okasaki, as described in the invaluable "Purely Functional Data Structures" (Cambridge University Press, ISBN 978-0521663502, 1998). Chapter 12 was inspired by a University of Cambridge Computer Science Tripos exam question set by Lawrence C. Paulson in 1999. Question 3 of that chapter is due to Peter D. Schumer in "Mathematical Journeys" (John Wiley & Sons, ISBN 0-471-22066-3, 2004).

I am grateful to the many colleagues and friends with whom I have been able to discuss OCaml style and substance, including Mark Shinwell, Leo White, Daniel Bünzli, Anil Madhavapeddy, Stephen Dolan and many others whom I have forgotten. Helpful comments on an earlier draft were provided by Stefan Schmiedl, Manuel Cornes, Jonas Bülow, Emmanuel Delaborde, Mario Alvarez Picallo, Giannis Tsaraias, Emmanuel Oga, and André Bjärby.

Summary of Basic OCaml

This chapter contains a summary of each OCaml construct used in the book, together with some examples. Pieces of OCaml syntax not contained in this chapter will be introduced as and when they are needed throughout the rest of the book. Existing OCaml programmers may skip this chapter.

Simple Data Types

Integers `min_int ... -3 -2 -1 0 1 2 3 ... max_int` of type **int**. Booleans `true` and `false` of type **bool**. Characters of type **char** like `'X'` and `'!'`.

Mathematical operators `+ - * / mod` which take two integers and give another.

$$6 * 2 \implies 12$$

Operators `= < <= > >= <>` which compare two values and evaluate to either `true` or `false`.

$$1 + 2 + 3 = 1 * 2 * 3 \implies \text{true}$$

The conditional **if** *expression1* **then** *expression2* **else** *expression3*, where *expresssion1* has type **bool** and *expression2* and *expression3* have the same type as one another.

$$\text{if } 4 * 3 > 2 * 2 \text{ then } 1 \text{ else } 0 \implies 1$$

The boolean operators && (logical AND) and || (logical OR) which allow us to build compound boolean expressions.

$$1 = 2 \,||\, 2 = 2 \implies \text{true}$$

Tuples to combine a fixed number of elements `(a, b)`, `(a, b, c)` etc. with types $\alpha \times \beta$, $\alpha \times \beta \times \gamma$ etc. For example, `(1, '1')` is a tuple of type **int** $\times$ **char**. On the screen, OCaml writes `'a` for α etc.

Strings, which are sequences of characters written between double quotes and are of type **string**. For example, `"one"` has type **string**.

Names and Functions

Assigning a name to the result of evaluating an expression using the **let** *name* = *expression* construct.

    `let x = 5 > 2`   *x is new, and is* `true`

Building compound expressions using **let** *name1* = *expression1* **in let** *name2* = *expression2* **in** ...

    `let x = 4 in let y = 5 in x + y`

Anonymous (un-named) functions **fun** *name* -> *expression*.

$$(\textbf{fun } x \text{ -> } x * 2) \; 4 \implies 8$$

Making operators into functions as in `( < )` and `( + )`.

$$(+) \; 1 \; 2 \implies 3$$

Functions, introduced by **let** *name argument1 argument2* ... = *expression*. These have type $\alpha \to \beta$, $\alpha \to \beta \to \gamma$ etc. for some types α, β, γ etc. For example, `let f a b = a > b` is a function of type $\alpha \to \alpha \to$ **bool**.

Recursive functions, which are introduced in the

same way, but using **let rec** instead of **let**. For example, here is a function g which calculates the smallest power of two greater than or equal to a given positive integer, using the recursive function f:

let rec f x y =
  if y < x **then** f x (2 * y) **else** y

let g z = f z 1

Mutually recursive functions, introduced by writing **let rec** f x = ... **and** g y = ... **and** ...

Pattern Matching

Matching patterns using **match** *expression1* **with** *pattern1* | ... -> *expression2* | *pattern2* | ... -> *expression3* | ... The expressions *expression2*, *expression3* etc. must have the same type as one another, and this is the type of the whole **match** ... **with** expression. The special pattern _ which matches anything.

match x **with**
  0 -> 1
| 1 | 2 -> 3
| _ -> 4

Matching two or more things at once, using commas to separate as in **match** a, b **with** 0, 0 -> *expression1* | x, y -> *expression2* | ...

match x, y, z **with**
  0, 0, 0 -> true
| _, _, _ -> false

Lists

Lists, which are ordered collections of zero or more elements of like type. They are written between square brackets, with elements separated by semicolons e.g. [1; 2; 3; 4; 5]. If a list is non-empty, it has a head, which is its first element, and a tail, which is the list composed of the rest of the elements.

The :: "cons" operator, which adds an element to the front of a list. The @ "append" operator, which concatenates two lists together.

1 :: [2; 3] $\Longrightarrow$ [1; 2; 3]
[1; 2] @ [3] $\Longrightarrow$ [1; 2; 3]

Lists and the :: "cons" symbol may be used for pattern matching to distinguish lists of length zero, one, etc. and with particular contents. For example, we can calculate the length of a list:

let rec length l =
  match l **with**
    [] -> 0
  | _::t -> 1 + length t

Exceptions

Defining exceptions with **exception** *name*. They can carry extra information by adding **of** *type*. Raising exceptions with **raise**. Handling exceptions with **try** ... **with** ...

exception Problem **of** int

let f x y =
  if y = 0
    then raise (Problem x)
    else x / y

let g x y =
  try f x y **with** Problem p -> p

Partial Application

Partial application of functions by giving fewer than the full number of arguments. Partial application with functions built from operators.

let add x y = x + y

List.map (add 3) [1; 2; 3]
$\Longrightarrow$ [4; 5; 6]

List.map ((+) 3) [1; 2; 3]
$\Longrightarrow$ [4; 5; 6]

New Data Types

New types with **type** *name* = *constructor1* **of** *type1* | *constructor2* **of** *type2* | ... Pattern matching on them as with the built-in types. Polymorphic types.

type colour =
  Red | Blue | Green | Grey **of** int

```
[Red; Blue; Grey 16]
```
this has type colour list

```
type 'a tree =
    Lf
  | Br of 'a tree * 'a * 'a tree
```

For example, `Br (Lf, 'X', Br (Lf, 'Y', Lf))` has type `char` tree. A useful built-in data type is the **option** type, defined as `type 'a option = None | Some of 'a`. A type can be polymorphic in more than one type parameter, for example `('a, 'b) Hashtbl.t`, as in the Standard Library.

Basic Input / Output

The value `()` and its type **unit**. Input channels of type **in_channel** and output channels of type **out_channel**. Built-in functions such as `open_in`, `close_in`, `open_out`, `close_out`, `input_char`, `output_char` etc. for reading from and writing to them respectively.

Mutable State

References of type α **ref**. Building them using `ref`, accessing their contents using `!` and updating them using the `:=` operator.

```
# let p = ref 0;;
val p : int ref = {contents = 0}
# p := 5;;
- : unit = ()
# !p;;
- : int = 5
```

Arrays of type α **array** written like `[|1; 2; 3|]`. Creating an array with the built-in function `Array.make`, finding its length with `Array.length`, accessing an element with `a.(subscript)`. Updating with `a.(subscript) <- expression`.

```
let swap a x y =
  let t = a.(x) in
    a.(x) <- a.(y); a.(y) <- t
```

Bracketing expressions together with **begin** and **end** instead of parentheses for readability.

```
if x = y then
  begin
    a := b;
    c := d
  end
else
  e := f
```

Performing an action many times based on a boolean condition with the **while** *boolean expression* **do** *expression* **done** construct.

```
while !x < y do x := !x * 2 done
```

Performing an action a fixed number of times with a varying parameter using the **for** *name = start* **to** *end* **do** *expression* **done** construct.

```
for x = 1 to 10 do print_int x done
```

Floating-point Numbers

Floating-point numbers `min_float` ... `max_float` of type **float**. Floating-point operators `+. *. -. /. **` and built-in functions `sqrt` `log` etc.

`2. ** 0.2` $\implies$ `1.1486983549970351`

The OCaml Standard Library

Using functions from the OCaml Standard Library with the form *Module.function*. For example, `List.map`, `String.length`, `Array.copy` etc. The **Buffer** module allows the efficient collation of strings into larger ones.

Simple Modules

Writing modules in `.ml` files. Building interfaces in `.mli` files with types and the **val** keyword. For example, the `.ml` file with contents `let f x = x + 1` might have the interface `val f : int -> int`

Compiling Programs

The `ocamlc` and `ocamlopt` compilers. For example:

`ocamlc -o x x.ml` builds x (or x.exe) from x.ml with the bytecode compiler.

`ocamlopt -o x x.ml` builds x (or x.exe) from x.ml with the native code compiler.

Our Working Environment

Every piece of code in an example, and every answer to an end-of-chapter question can be downloaded from the book's website at http://www.ocaml-book.com/ and built on the reader's machine. The programs work on Unix (including Linux), Mac OS X, and Microsoft Windows, using OCaml 4.02 or later.

Since several of our programs require tail-recursive list functions, we provide a wrapper to the Standard Library **List** module which provides them. In addition, three small utility functions (take, drop, and from) are provided in a Util module. These modules are contained in the module More. So, by writing **open** More, the Util module is available, and all functions in the **List** module are tail-recursive.

If using OPAM, the OCaml Package Manager, this package may be installed by writing opam install more-ocaml. Then (or by installing in another manner – see the online resources for details) our modules are available in the top level:

```
        OCaml

# #use "topfind";;
- : unit = ()
Findlib has been successfully loaded. Additional directives:
  #require "package";;      to load a package
  #list;;                   to list the available packages
  #camlp4o;;                to load camlp4 (standard syntax)
  #camlp4r;;                to load camlp4 (revised syntax)
  #predicates "p,q,...";;   to set these predicates
  Topfind.reset();;         to force that packages will be reloaded
  #thread;;                 to enable threads

- : unit = ()
# #require "more";;
/Users/john/.opam/4.02.0/lib/ocaml/more.cma: loaded
/Users/john/.opam/4.02.0/lib/more: added to search path
# open More;;
# Util.take;;
- : 'a list -> int -> 'a list = <fun>
```

They are also available when compiling stand-alone programs with the bytecode compiler ocamlc or the native code compiler ocamlopt:

```
ocamlfind ocamlc -package more program.ml -linkpkg -o program
ocamlfind ocamlopt -package more program.ml -linkpkg -o program
```

Further instructions, including for use on platforms where OPAM is not supported, are given in the online resources.

Timing with the Unix module

Sometimes we will wish to see how much time a piece of code takes. This can be achieved using the function `gettimeofday` from the **Unix** module (contrary to its name, this module also works on Windows). This function returns a floating-point number representing the time since 00:00:00 GMT, Jan. 1, 1970, in seconds:

```
        OCaml
# #use "topfind";;
- : unit = ()
Findlib has been successfully loaded. Additional directives:
  #require "package";;      to load a package
  #list;;                   to list the available packages
  #camlp4o;;                to load camlp4 (standard syntax)
  #camlp4r;;                to load camlp4 (revised syntax)
  #predicates "p,q,...";;   to set these predicates
  Topfind.reset();;         to force that packages will be reloaded
  #thread;;                 to enable threads

- : unit = ()
# #require "unix";;
/Users/john/.opam/4.01.0/lib/ocaml/unix.cma: loaded
# Unix.gettimeofday ();;
- : float = 1407679005.43897
# Unix.gettimeofday ();;
- : float = 1407679011.08860302
```

Now, by evaluating `Unix.gettimeofday ()`, running a piece of code, and evaluating `Unix.gettimeofday ()` once more, we can calculate the elapsed time. To use the **Unix** module when compiling stand-alone programs:

```
ocamlfind ocamlc -package more,unix program.ml -linkpkg -o program
ocamlfind ocamlopt -package more,unix program.ml -linkpkg -o program
```

Coping with Errors

Finding and fixing errors is an inevitable part of programming. A short guide to the most common errors and how to deal with them has been included on page 195.

Chapter 1

Unravelling "Fold"

The **List** module in OCaml's Standard Library defines two intriguingly-named functions over lists:

```
fold_left  : (α → β → α) → α → β list → α
fold_right : (α → β → β) → α list → β → β

let rec fold_left f a l =
  match l with
    [] -> a
  | h::t -> fold_left f (f a h) t

let rec fold_right f l a =
  match l with
    [] -> a
  | h::t -> f h (fold_right f t a)
```

What do they do? And why are they considered important enough to include in the Standard Library? As we shall see, they abstract the idea of recursion over lists with an accumulator in a most delightfully generic way.

Let us first examine `fold_left` and its rather complicated type. The first argument is itself a function, which takes the existing accumulator and an element from the input list, combines them in some fashion, and returns a new accumulator, ready for the next element. So, in general, the first argument has type $\alpha \to \beta \to \alpha$. Then we have an initial value for the accumulator, which must have type α, and an input list of type β **list**. The return value is the final accumulator, so that must have type α. We can annotate the function as follows:

```
fold_left : (α → β → α) → α → β list → α

let rec fold_left f a l =                function, initial accumulator, input list
  match l with
    [] -> a                              no more input – return the accumulator
  | h::t -> fold_left f (f a h) t        apply function to a and h, making new a
```

We can find the sum of a list of numbers:

$$\begin{array}{rl} & \texttt{fold\_left (+) 0 [1; 2; 3]} \\ \implies & \texttt{fold\_left (+) 1 [2; 3]} \\ \implies & \texttt{fold\_left (+) 3 [3]} \\ \implies & \texttt{fold\_left (+) 6 []} \\ \implies & 6 \end{array}$$

Here, α and β are both **int**. The function (+) has the right type, and we use for the initial accumulator the *identity element* for (+) which is 0 since for all x, $x + 0 = x$ (we cannot take the initial accumulator from the list itself since our function must have a result for the sum of all the integers in an empty list.)

It might appear to the reader that this is more complicated than the simple recursive solution, but to the experienced functional programmer, using `fold_left` is in fact *easier* to read. Let us find the maximum number in a list using `fold_left`:

$$\begin{array}{rl} & \texttt{fold\_left max min\_int [2; 4; 6; 0; 1]} \\ \implies & \texttt{fold\_left max 2 [4; 6; 0; 1]} \\ \implies & \texttt{fold\_left max 4 [6; 0; 1]} \\ \implies & \texttt{fold\_left max 6 [0; 1]} \\ \implies & \texttt{fold\_left max 6 [1]} \\ \implies & \texttt{fold\_left max 6 []} \\ \implies & 6 \end{array}$$

Here `max` is the built-in function for finding the larger of two things, and `min_int` is the built-in value of the smallest possible integer. We can use a similar scheme to define functions on lists of booleans:

```
all : bool list → bool
any : bool list → bool

let all l = fold_left ( && ) true l

let any l = fold_left ( || ) false l
```

The `all` function is true if and only if all items in the list are true; the `any` function if at least one is. What can happen when α and β are different? How about making the accumulator a list too? We can use `List.mem` to turn an arbitrary list into a set by consulting the existing accumulator before putting an element in:

```
setify : α list → α list

let setify l =
   fold_left (fun a e -> if List.mem e a then a else e :: a) [] l
```

We are using `List.mem` to decide whether to add each element to the accumulator or discard it.

What about `fold_right`?

Here is the function again:

```
fold_right : (α → β → β) → α list → β → β

let rec fold_right f l a =
  match l with
    [] -> a
  | h::t -> f h (fold_right f t a)
```

The `fold_left` function applied the given function over the elements in the input list from the left hand side. In contrast, `fold_right` processes them from the right, by changing the evaluation order. Consider, for example, our summation example:

$$
\begin{aligned}
&\quad\ \text{fold\_left (+) 0 [1; 2; 3]} \\
\Longrightarrow &\quad\ \text{fold\_left (+) 1 [2; 3]} \\
\Longrightarrow &\quad\ \text{fold\_left (+) 3 [3]} \\
\Longrightarrow &\quad\ \text{fold\_left (+) 6 []} \\
\Longrightarrow &\quad\ 6
\end{aligned}
$$

$$
\begin{aligned}
&\quad\ \text{fold\_right (+) [1; 2; 3] 0} \\
\Longrightarrow &\quad\ \text{(+) 1 (fold\_right (+) [2; 3] 0)} \\
\Longrightarrow &\quad\ \text{(+) 1 ((+) 2 (fold\_right (+) [3] 0))} \\
\Longrightarrow &\quad\ \text{(+) 1 ((+) 2 ((+) 3 (fold\_right (+) [] 0)))} \\
\Longrightarrow &\quad\ \text{(+) 1 ((+) 2 ((+) 3 0))} \\
\Longrightarrow &\quad\ \text{(+) 1 ((+) 2 3)} \\
\Longrightarrow &\quad\ \text{(+) 1 5} \\
\Longrightarrow &\quad\ 6
\end{aligned}
$$

See how the accumulating of values starts from the right hand side. Note also that `fold_right` is not tail-recursive (the intermediate expression it builds is proportional to the size of the input). We can define map simply as a use of `fold_right`.

```
map : (α → β) → α list → β list

let map f l =
  fold_right (fun e a -> f e :: a) l []
```

Who would have thought that `fold_right` was the more fundamental function? At the cost of a list reversal, we can make `fold_right` tail-recursive by defining it in terms of `fold_left`:

```
fold_right : (α → β → β) → α list → β → β

let fold_right f l e =
  fold_left (fun x y -> f y x) e (List.rev l)
```

Sometimes we want to provide an initial accumulator value which is not the identity element for the computation. For example, applying :: over an input list with `fold_right` is not very interesting, yielding a function which returns a copy of its input:

```
copy : α list → α list

let copy l =
  fold_right (fun e a -> e :: a) l []
```

But if we supply a non-empty list as the initial value of the accumulator, we have the `append` function:

```
append : α list → α list → α list

let append x y =
  fold_right (fun e a -> e :: a) x y
```

We can use a more complicated accumulator, such as a tuple. In this example, we replicate the `List.split` function which, given a list of pairs, yields a pair of lists:

```
split : (α × β) list → α list × β list

let split l =
  fold_right
    (fun (x, y) (xs, ys) -> (x :: xs, y :: ys))
    l
    ([], [])
```

For example, `split [(1, "one"); (2, "two")]` evaluates to `([1; 2], ["one"; "two"])`.

A word of caution

One very simple definition for the function `concat` which concatenates all lists in a list of lists is given by:

```
concat : α list list → α list

let concat l = fold_left ( @ ) [] l
```

We use the append function to accumulate the lists into a single list one by one:

$$\begin{aligned}
&\texttt{fold\_left (@) [] [[1;2]; [3]; [4;5]]} \\
\Longrightarrow\ &\texttt{fold\_left (@) [1; 2] [[3]; [4; 5]]} \\
\Longrightarrow\ &\texttt{fold\_left (@) [1; 2; 3] [[4; 5]]} \\
\Longrightarrow\ &\texttt{fold\_left (@) [1; 2; 3; 4; 5] []} \\
\Longrightarrow\ &\texttt{[1; 2; 3; 4; 5]}
\end{aligned}$$

However, the order of evaluation is such that the append function @ (which takes time proportional to the length of its first argument) is used inefficiently – we process the list again and again.

Folding over trees

For the usual definition of a binary tree, we can define a fold. There are two accumulators, one for everything from the left sub-tree, and one for everything from the right sub-tree. The supplied function combines both into a new accumulator.

$\texttt{fold\_tree} : (\alpha \to \beta \to \beta \to \beta) \to \beta \to \alpha\ \textbf{tree} \to \beta$

```
type 'a tree =
    Lf
  | Br of 'a * 'a tree * 'a tree

let rec fold_tree f e t =
  match t with
    Lf -> e
  | Br (x, l, r) -> f x (fold_tree f e l) (fold_tree f e r)
```

Here is an example tree:

which we write as   `Br (1, Br (0, Lf, Lf), Br (6, Br (4, Lf, Lf), Lf))`

Functions for the size of a tree, and the sum of an integer tree are now easy, without explicit recursion:

```
tree_size : α tree → int
tree_sum  : int tree → int

let tree_size t = fold_tree (fun _ l r -> 1 + l + r) 0 t

let tree_sum t = fold_tree (fun x l r -> x + l + r) 0 t
```

The standard tree traversals can be written easily with a list accumulator. A little typographical manipulation shows the pleasing symmetry:

```
tree_preorder  : α tree → α list
tree_inorder   : α tree → α list
tree_postorder : α tree → α list

let tree_preorder  t = fold_tree (fun x l r -> [x] @ l @ r) [] t
let tree_inorder   t = fold_tree (fun x l r -> l @ [x] @ r) [] t
let tree_postorder t = fold_tree (fun x l r -> l @ r @ [x]) [] t
```

On our example list:

$\quad$ tree_preorder (Br (1, Br (0, Lf, Lf), Br (6, Br (4, Lf, Lf), Lf)))
$\implies$ [1; 0; 6; 4]

$\quad$ tree_inorder (Br (1, Br (0, Lf, Lf), Br (6, Br (4, Lf, Lf), Lf)))
$\implies$ [0; 1; 4; 6]

$\quad$ tree_postorder (Br (1, Br (0, Lf, Lf), Br (6, Br (4, Lf, Lf), Lf)))
$\implies$ [0; 4; 6; 1]

Questions

1. Write a function which, given a list of integers representing expenses, removes them from a budget, again represented by an integer.
2. Calculate the length of a list using one of the `fold_` functions.
3. Use one of the `fold_` functions to find the last element of list, if any. Behave sensibly if the list is empty.
4. Write a function to reverse a list, using one of the `fold_` functions.
5. Write a version of `List.mem` using one of the `fold_` functions. Now `setify` can be defined entirely using folds.
6. Use a fold to write a function which, given a list of non-empty strings representing words, returns a single string where the words are separated by spaces. Comment on its efficiency.
7. Use `fold_tree` to write a function which calculates the maximum depth of a tree. What is its type?
8. Compare the time efficiency of one or more of your functions with the system implementation of the same function (for example, our fold-based member function vs. `List.mem`) with regard to both computational complexity and actual time taken.
9. Comment on whether the use of folds in each of Questions 1–7 is good style.

Chapter 2

Being Lazy

We can make our own data type for OCaml's built-in lists like this:

```
type 'a list = Nil | Cons of 'a * 'a list
```

The constructor `Nil` represents the empty list, and `Cons` builds a list from a head and a tail. So, for example, we can write the list [1; 2; 3] as `Cons (1, Cons (2, Cons (3, Nil)))`. It is also possible to define an infinitely-long list, where elements are only produced when we actually need them. This is known as a *lazy list*. Instead of a tail, we use a *tail function*. This is a function which, when given a unit value, yields the tail:

```
type 'a lazylist = Cons of 'a * (unit -> 'a lazylist)
```

Note that we have no `Nil` constructor, because the list has no end. Our use of **unit** rather than another type is a choice – we could use any type, but **unit** is the simplest type, containing only one value. How do we use such a creature? Let us start by writing a function which, given an integer n, builds the lazy list of all integers $n, n+1, n+2\ldots$ and returns it:

---

lseq : int → int lazylist

let rec lseq n =
　Cons (n, **fun** () -> lseq (n + 1))

When we type this in to the OCaml top level, here is what we see:

OCaml

```
# lseq 0;;
- : int lazylist = Cons (0, <fun>)
```

We can see that the head of the list is zero – the rest is yet to be calculated. OCaml represents the tail function with `<fun>`. We can now write functions to extract items from the list. Here are lazy head and tail functions:

```
lhd  :  α lazylist → α
ltl  :  α lazylist → α lazylist

let lhd (Cons (n, _)) = n

let ltl (Cons (_, tf)) = tf ()
```

Notice that, because there is only one constructor in our data type, we can pattern match directly in the function argument. When we apply the unit () to the tail function, we are *forcing evaluation* of the tail. Here are lazy versions of the familiar `take` and `drop` functions, which take or drop the first n elements of a list:

```
ltake  :  α lazylist → int → α list
ldrop  :  α lazylist → int → α lazylist

let rec ltake (Cons (h, tf)) n =
  match n with
    0 -> []
  | _ -> h :: ltake (tf ()) (n - 1)

let rec ldrop (Cons (h, tf) as ll) n =
  match n with
    0 -> ll
  | _ -> ldrop (tf ()) (n - 1)
```

The `ltake` function has to yield an ordinary list, of course. Note the use of the **as** keyword to name part of the pattern (here, `Cons (h, tf)` is named `ll`), making the base case of `ldrop` simpler. Now we can actually get at our elements:

OCaml

```
# ltake (lseq 0) 20;;
- : int list =
[0; 1; 2; 3; 4; 5; 6; 7; 8; 9; 10; 11; 12; 13; 14; 15; 16; 17; 18; 19]
# ldrop (lseq 0) 20;;
- : int lazylist = Cons (20, <fun>)
```

Two favourite list functions have easy analogues in the lazy world:

Chapter 2. Being Lazy

```
lmap    : (α → β) → α lazylist → β lazylist
lfilter : (α → bool) → α lazylist → α lazylist

let rec lmap f (Cons (h, tf)) =
  Cons (f h, fun () -> lmap f (tf ()))

let rec lfilter f (Cons (h, tf)) =
  if f h then
    Cons (h, fun () -> lfilter f (tf ()))
  else
    lfilter f (tf ())
```

Note that delaying and forcing evaluation often come together, as in both these examples. The function map returns almost immediately – assuming f is quick. The computation of the rest of the elements is, as always, delayed. The filter function is different – it must find at least one matching element to use as the head, before returning. If it does not find one, it will never return, so care is needed. Let us use these two functions to find the cubes divisible by five:

```
cubes : int lazylist

let cubes =
  lfilter
    (fun x -> x mod 5 = 0)
    (lmap (fun x -> x * x * x) (lseq 1))
```

Now, using ltake:

OCaml

```
# ltake cubes 20;;
- : int list =
[125; 1000; 3375; 8000; 15625; 27000; 42875; 64000; 91125; 125000; 166375;
 216000; 274625; 343000; 421875; 512000; 614125; 729000; 857375; 1000000]
```

Here is another example of a simple lazy list, this time the list of all primes, created by use of lfilter and recursion, beginning with the list of all numbers from 2, calculated with lseq:

```
mkprimes : int lazylist → int lazylist
primes   : int lazylist

let rec mkprimes (Cons (h, tf)) =
  Cons (h, fun () ->
    mkprimes (lfilter (fun x -> x mod h <> 0) (tf ())))

let primes = mkprimes (lseq 2)
```

There are plenty of list functions which cannot be adapted to lazy lists. We cannot, for example, reverse a lazy list, or append two lazy lists. But there is an analogue to append. We can combine two lists fairly, taking elements in turn from each:

```
interleave : α lazylist → α lazylist → α lazylist

let rec interleave (Cons (h, tf)) l =
  Cons (h, fun () -> interleave l (tf ()))
```

For example, the list alternating between zeros and ones can be built with interleave and a function to build constant lists:

```
lconst : int → int lazylist
interleaved : int lazylist

let rec lconst n =
  Cons (n, fun () -> lconst n)

let interleaved =
  interleave (lconst 0) (lconst 1)
```

A more interesting example is to calculate the lazy list of all ordinary lists of zeros and ones. We can do this by prepending a zero and a one to the list, and interleaving the resulting lists:

```
allfrom : int list → int list lazylist
allones : int list lazylist

let rec allfrom l =
  Cons (l, fun () ->
    interleave (allfrom (0 :: l)) (allfrom (1 :: l)))

let allones = allfrom []
```

This yields:

OCaml

```
# ltake allones 20;;
- : int list list =
[[]; [0]; [1]; [0; 0]; [0; 1]; [1; 0]; [1; 1]; [0; 0; 0]; [0; 0; 1];
 [0; 1; 0]; [0; 1; 1]; [1; 0; 0]; [1; 0; 1]; [1; 1; 0]; [1; 1; 1];
 [0; 0; 0; 0]; [0; 0; 0; 1]; [0; 0; 1; 0]; [0; 0; 1; 1]; [0; 1; 0; 0]]
```

To see why, we can visualise the evaluation as a tree where each left branch prepends a zero and each right branch a one:

```
                    [ ]
                 ╱       ╲
              [0]         [1]
             ╱   ╲       ╱   ╲
         [0; 0] [1; 0] [0; 1] [1; 1]
         ╱ ╲   ╱ ╲    ╱ ╲   ╱ ╲
```

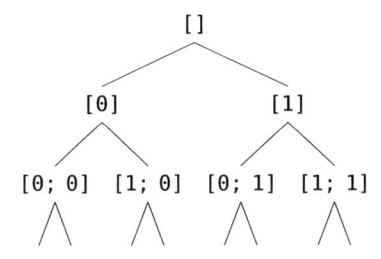

The interleavings are fair, and the interleavings of interleavings equally so, thus we see the results of length two in this order: [0; 0] [0; 1] [1; 0] [1; 1].

Questions

1. Write the lazy list whose elements are the numbers $1, 2, 4, 8, 16\ldots$ What is its type?

2. Write a function to return the nth element of a lazy list where element zero is the head of the list.

3. Write a function which, given a list, returns the lazy list forming a repeated sequence taken from that list. For example, given the list [1; 2; 3] it should return a lazy list with elements $1, 2, 3, 1, 2, 3, 1, 2\ldots$

4. Write a lazy list whose elements are the fibonacci numbers $0, 1, 1, 2, 3, 5, 8\ldots$ whose first two elements are zero and one by definition, and each ensuing element is the sum of the previous two.

5. Write the function `unleave` which, given a lazy list, returns two lazy lists, one containing elements at positions $0, 2, 4, 6\ldots$ of the original list, and the other containing elements at positions $1, 3, 5, 7\ldots$

6. Alphanumeric labels in documents go $A, B, C, \ldots, X, Y, Z, AA, AB, \ldots, BA, BB, \ldots AAA, \ldots$ Write the lazy list containing strings representing this sequence. You may (mis)use the Standard Library function `Char.escaped` to convert a character to a string.

Chapter 3

Named Tuples with Records

Tuples can be used to combine a fixed number of elements of same or differing types. However, once we have more than two or three items, remembering the order can be difficult, especially if the types of the items are the same. *Records* remedy this, allowing us to name each item. Due to this naming, they have several other useful properties which distinguish them from tuples. Let us define a simple type for cartesian coordinates in two dimensions:

```
type point = {x : float; y : float}
```

Records are like tuples with labels. We write them between braces { }. Each element of the record (called a *field*) has a name and a type, and the fields are separated with semicolons. We can construct a value of this type using the same syntax, but with the equals sign in place of the colons:

```
let p = {x = 4.5; y = 6.0}
```

We can add another field to the record, a label for the point:

```
type point = {x : float; y : float; label : string}
```

We can parametrize it just like a list or variant data type:

```
type 'a point =
  {x : float;
   y : float;
   label : string;
   content : 'a}
```

So now we can have values of type **int** point and **string** point and so on. We can define one directly:

```
p : int list point
make_point : float → float → string → α → α point

let p =
  {x = 4.5;
   y = 6.0;
   label = "P";
   content = [1; 3; 1]}

let make_point x y l c =
  {x = x; y = y; label = l; content = c}
```

Notice that frequently we write something like x = x in a record definition, as in make_point here. This can be shortened to just x, and by doing so for all the arguments in make_point we obtain this simpler definition:

```
make_point : float → float → string → α → α point

let make_point x y label content =
  {x; y; label; content}
```

Having built record values, we now need to know how to extract the individual parts. We can use the dot notation, writing *record.field* like so:

```
string_of_point : α point → string

let string_of_point p =
  p.label
  ^ " = ("
  ^ string_of_float p.x
  ^ ", "
  ^ string_of_float p.y
  ^ ")"
```

Alternatively, we can use record syntax in patterns, here in the argument itself:

```
string_of_point : α point → string

let string_of_point {label = l; x = x; y = y} =
  l
  ^ " = ("
  ^ string_of_float x
  ^ ", "
  ^ string_of_float y
  ^ ")"
```

Notice we only had to include in the pattern the parts of the record we intended to use. This can, optionally, be made more explicit by adding the wildcard _ to the pattern:

```
string_of_point : α point → string

let string_of_point {label = l; x = x; y = y; _} =
  l
  ^ " = ("
  ^ string_of_float x
  ^ ", "
  ^ string_of_float y
  ^ ")"
```

Finally, we can use the shorthand record form in patterns too:

```
string_of_point : α point → string

let string_of_point {label; x; y; _} =
  label
  ^ " = ("
  ^ string_of_float x
  ^ ", "
  ^ string_of_float y
  ^ ")"
```

Where we need a copy of a record with just one or more fields changed, we can use the **with** keyword:

```
relabel : α point → string → α point

let relabel p l = {p with label = l}
```

Again, the shortened form can help:

```
relabel : α point → string → α point

let relabel p label = {p with label}
```

Here is a function to reflect a point about the line $x = y$:

```
mirror : α point → α point

let mirror p = {p with x = p.y; y = p.x}
```

Mutable records

Individual fields of a record can be made mutable (their value may be changed – literally mutated), by use of the **mutable** keyword:

```
type 'a point =
  {x : float;
   y : float;
   label : string;
   mutable content : 'a}
```

In fact, OCaml's reference type is just a record with a single, mutable field:

OCaml

```
# let x = ref 0;;
- : int ref = { contents = 0 }
```

Here, the type **ref** is defined by **type** 'a ref = {**mutable** contents : 'a} and the constructor function ref is of type $\alpha \to \alpha$ **ref**. The value of a mutable field can be updated using the <- symbol like this:

OCaml

```
# type 'a point = {x : float; y : float; label : string; mutable content : 'a};;
type 'a point = {
  x : float;
  y : float;
  label : string;
  mutable content : 'a;
}

# let p = {x = 4.5; y = 6.0; label = "P"; content = [1; 3; 1]};;
val p : int list point = {x = 4.5; y = 6.; label = "P"; content = [1; 3; 1]}

# p.content <- [1];;
- : unit = ()

# p;;
- : int list point = {x = 4.5; y = 6.; label = "P"; content = [1]}
```

Such records should be used with care, like any mutable feature, especially if they are likely to be used as part of a larger data structure.

Questions

1. Show how to update a reference without using the := operator.

2. Using functions from the "Time Functions" section of the documentation to the **Unix** module, write a program which, when run, returns a string containing the time and date, for example `"It is 2:45 on Wednesday 8 January 2014"`.

3. What is the difference between **type** t = {x : int ref} and **type** t = {**mutable** x : int}? What are the advantages and disadvantages of each?

4. Define a record of six items $a...f$ where a and b have the same type as one another, c and d have the same type as one another and e and f have the same type as one another.

5. Records are used in the module **Gc** which controls OCaml's garbage collector (a garbage collector is a system which automatically reclaims space the program has finished with as the program is running). Use the data structures and functions in the **Gc** module to write programs which:

    (a) write a summary of the state of the garbage collector to a text file; and

    (b) alter the verbosity of the garbage collector as defined in the `control` record.

Chapter 4

Generalized Input/Output

In **Pervasives**, OCaml's default always-opened module, a number of functions are defined over input and output *channels* – representing both files in the file system and special ones such as standard output. However, it is often useful to have a more general abstraction of input and output over, for example, strings and arrays, as well as files and channels.

In this chapter, we shall develop such an abstraction, giving input and output types which work with OCaml channels and strings. It can be extended to work over other data structures, and to have more complete functionality – some of the questions at the end of the chapter involve such extensions.

A type for inputs

The fundamental operations on an input, once it has been created, will be:

- finding the current position;
- setting the current position;
- reading a character, at the same time advancing the position;
- finding the length of an input.

We need a way to group them together, and to refer to them easily. A record is ideal:

```
type input =
  {pos_in : unit -> int;
   seek_in : int -> unit;
   input_char : unit -> char;
   in_channel_length : int}
```

Now we can build an input from an OCaml **in_channel** easily (we have re-used some of the standard OCaml names):

```
input_of_channel : in_channel → input

let input_of_channel ch =
  {pos_in = (fun () -> pos_in ch);
   seek_in = seek_in ch;
   input_char = (fun () -> input_char ch);
   in_channel_length = in_channel_length ch}
```

Notice that the original channel is now hidden inside the input – the functions `pos_in` and `input_char` instead simply take the unit `()` as their input. Let us assure ourselves that this structure also works for abstracting over strings:

```
input_of_string : string → input

let input_of_string s =
  let pos = ref 0 in
    {pos_in = (fun () -> !pos);
     seek_in =
       (fun p ->
         if p < 0 then
           raise (Invalid_argument "seek before beginning");
         pos := p);
     input_char =
       (fun () ->
         if !pos > String.length s - 1
           then raise End_of_file
           else (let c = s.[!pos] in pos := !pos + 1; c));
     in_channel_length = String.length s}
```

We allocate a local reference, `pos`, to hold the current position. It cannot be accessed directly, only manipulated through the exposed record of functions. The `pos_in` and `in_channel_length` functions are simple. The `seek_in` function needs to check that the position is positive, but we allow it to be beyond the end, for compatibility with OCaml channels. The `input_char` function checks it is not trying to read beyond the end of the string, then reads a character, advances the position, and returns the character.

Notice we use the same exception scheme as OCaml does in its own channels – raising `End_of_file` if a read is attempted beyond the last character.

Example: reading words

We should like to write a program which can extract the words from a given input, such as a string or a file. For example, given the string

    "There were four of them; more than before."

we wish to produce

    ["there"; "were"; "four"; "of"; "them"; "more"; "than"; "before"]

Chapter 4. Generalized Input/Output

removing spaces, punctuation and making the words lower case. First, let us define a function to rewind the input by one character (useful when we have read a character and decided we do not wish to consume it), and another, a predicate to determine if a character is considered a non-letter, and thus may be skipped:

```
rewind : input → unit
is_non_letter : char → bool

let rewind i =
  i.seek_in (i.pos_in () - 1)

let is_non_letter x =
  match x with
    ' ' | '!' | '(' | ')' | '.' | ',' | ';' | ':' -> true
  | _ -> false
```

Now, we can write a function `skip_characters` to skip any punctuation from the current point. It may raise End_of_file, of course. Then, we have the function `collect_characters` which, given a fresh **Buffer.t** and an input which has been processed by `skip_characters`, returns the string containing the next sequence of interesting characters, or raises End_of_file if we are at the end of the input.

```
skip_characters : input → unit
collect_characters : input → string

let rec skip_characters i =
  if is_non_letter (i.input_char ())
    then skip_characters i
    else rewind i

let rec collect_characters b i =
  match
    try Some (i.input_char ()) with End_of_file -> None
  with
    None -> Buffer.contents b
  | Some c ->
      if is_non_letter c
        then Buffer.contents b
        else (Buffer.add_char b c; collect_characters b i)
```

Finally, we can write `read_word` which finds the next word, if there is one. Then `read_words` collects them all in a list, and turns them in to lower case using the Standard Library function `String.lowercase`. These functions form Figure 4.1. For example:

```
# read_words (input_of_string "There were four of them; more than before.");;
- : string list = ["there"; "were"; "four"; "of"; "them"; "more"; "than"; "before"]
```

```
read_word : input → string option
read_words_inner : input → string list → string list
read_words : input → string list

let read_word i =
  try
    skip_characters i;
    Some (collect_characters (Buffer.create 20) i)
  with
    End_of_file -> None

let rec read_words_inner i a =
  match read_word i with
    None -> List.rev (List.map String.lowercase a)
  | Some w -> read_words_inner i (w :: a)

let read_words i =
  read_words_inner i []
```

Figure 4.1

A type for outputs

What do we need for a generic output? We must have an `output_char` function to write a single character, at least. It is also useful to have an `out_channel_length` function so we know how many characters have been written. We will not allow seeking back and forth like with our input type for the sake of simplicity. Figure 4.2 shows the output type, and functions to build outputs from channels and strings.

The **bytes** type in OCaml is for mutable strings. Mutable means we can change individual characters within the **bytes** string, but not its length. Strings of type **string** are, in modern versions of OCaml, immutable. The following functions from the `Bytes` module are useful:

Function	Type	Description
create	int → bytes	Create a **bytes** of given length, with arbitrary contents.
length	bytes → int	Return the length of a **bytes**.
get	bytes → int → char	Get the character at a given location.
set	bytes → int → char → unit	Set the character at a given location.
of_string	string → bytes	Make a new **bytes** with the same contents as a given **string**.
to_string	bytes → string	Make a new **string** with the same contents as a given **bytes**.

Note that whilst we have unified the interface for writing to mutable strings and channels, they remain different things: the string has limited, fixed length, and if the length is not all used it will contain junk at the end. Let us use these functions to build a function which writes a list of integers to any output:

Chapter 4. Generalized Input/Output

```
output_of_channel : out_channel → output
output_of_bytes : bytes → output

type output =
  {output_char : char -> unit;
   out_channel_length : unit -> int}

let output_of_channel ch =
  {output_char = (fun c -> output_byte ch (int_of_char c));
   out_channel_length = (fun () -> out_channel_length ch)}

let output_of_bytes b =
  let pos = ref 0 in
    {output_char =
      (fun c ->
        if !pos < Bytes.length b
          then (Bytes.set b !pos c; pos := !pos + 1)
          else raise End_of_file);
     out_channel_length =
       (fun () -> Bytes.length b)}
```

Figure 4.2

```
output_int_list : output → int list → unit

let output_int_list o ls =
  o.output_char '[';
  List.iter
    (fun n ->
      String.iter o.output_char (string_of_int n);
      o.output_char ';';
      o.output_char ' ')
    ls;
  o.output_char ']'
```

Note that `o.output_char` has an appropriate type for use with standard functions such as `String.iter`. We can test with an output built from standard output:

```
# output_int_list (output_of_channel stdout) [1; 2; 3; 4; 5];;
[1; 2; 3; 4; 5 ]
- : unit = ()
```

Can you find a way to suppress the extraneous space before the] character?

Questions

1. Write a function to build an input from an array of characters.
2. Write a function `input_string` of type **input** → **int** → **string** which returns the given number of characters from the input as a string, or fewer if the input has ended.
3. Extend the input type to include a function `input_char_opt` which returns a value of type **char option**, with None signalling end of file. Extend the functions `input_of_channel` and `input_of_string` appropriately.
4. Extend the input type with a function `input_byte` which returns an integer representing the next byte, or the special value −1 at end of file. Comment on the usefulness of this compared with `input_char_opt` and `input_char`.
5. Write an input type which raises `End_of_file` if it reaches a new line (a '\n' character). Use this to build a program which reads a line from standard input.
6. Write a function to build an output from a **Buffer.t**. Show how this can be used to retrieve a final string after output is finished.

Chapter 5

Streams of Bits

We have dealt with byte-by-byte streams of information. Often, though, we need to consider data as a stream of bits. Can we build a nice abstraction for this?

We could start with a function which builds a list of bits from a byte, and use that for each byte in the stream, building a final list. This has two disadvantages: it is inefficient in space and time (there are eight times as many bits as bytes, of course), and it processes all the bytes at once, rather than as required. Instead, let us build a bit stream based on our input type:

```
type input_bits =
  {input : input;
   mutable byte : int;
   mutable bit : int}
```

The `input` field is the input this bit stream is based upon. It will start from the most significant bit of the current byte of that input. The `byte` field holds the byte just read from the input, or an undefined value if no byte has yet been read. The `bit` field records the current bit position, but instead of 0..7 we will use 128, 64, 32, 16, 8, 4, 2, 1 so this field can be used directly to extract the bit using the built-in logical AND operator `land`, and then halved:

0	1	2	3	4	5	6	7	8	9	10	11	12	13	14	15	16	17	18	19	20	21	22	23	24	25	26	
0	1	1	1	0	1	1	0	1	1	1	0	0	0	1	1	0	1	1	0	0	1	1	0	0	0	0	input data
0b01110110								0b11100011								0b01100110								0b000...			value of byte
128	64	32	16	8	4	2	1	128	64	32	16	8	4	2	1	128	64	32	16	8	4	2	1	128	64	32	value of bits
F	T	T	T	F	T	T	F	T	T	T	F	F	F	T	T	F	T	T	F	F	T	T	F	F	F	F	byte land bits > 0

The expression `x land y` where x and y are integers yields an integer whose value has a bit pattern which is the bitwise logical AND of x and y. This `input_bits` type can be wholly abstracted, defined in the `.mli` by just **type** input_bits. Now, we can define a function to build an input_bits from an input:

27

```
input_bits_of_input : input → input_bits

let input_bits_of_input i =
  {input = i;
   byte = 0;
   bit = 0}
```

The function to get the next bit is simple. If bit is zero, we must load a new byte from the input and return the next bit. If bit is non-zero, we extract the given bit, and halve bit ready for next time.

```
getbit : input_bits → bool

let rec getbit b =
  if b.bit = 0 then
    begin
      b.byte <- int_of_char (b.input.input_char ());
      b.bit <- 128;
      getbit b
    end
  else
    let r = b.byte land b.bit > 0 in
      b.bit <- b.bit / 2;
      r
```

This function can raise End_of_file, of course, if the underlying call to input_char raises it. Two other functions are useful. We can align the bit stream on the next byte boundary trivially:

```
align : input_bits → unit

let align b =
  b.bit <- 0
```

We can write a function getval to return a given number of bits considered as an integer, allowing us to read a data field of any width. We use the lor operator, which gives the bitwise logical OR of two integers, and the lsl or *logical shift left* operator, which shifts the bits in an integer left by the specified number of bits, filling zeros on the right.

Chapter 5. Streams of Bits

```
getval : input_bits → int → int

let getval b n =
  if n <= 0 || n > 31 then
    raise (Invalid_argument "getval")
  else
    let r = ref 0 in
      for x = n - 1 downto 0 do
        r := !r lor ((if getbit b then 1 else 0) lsl x)
      done;
      !r
```

OCaml integers are at least 31 bits (depending upon the computer), so we can read fields up to 31 bits wide with this function. This number on a particular computer can be calculated by evaluating `Sys.word_size - 1`.

Example: decoding a TCP datagram header

Here is the layout of the header of a datagram of the TCP (Transmission Control Protocol) used for network communications:

0 1 2 3	4 5 6 7 8 9 10 11 12 13 14 15	16 17 18 19 20 21 22 23 24 25 26 27 28 29 30 31
\multicolumn{2}{c	}{Source port}	Destination port
\multicolumn{3}{c	}{Sequence number}
\multicolumn{3}{c	}{Acknowledgment number}
Data offset	Reserved · URG · ACK · PSH · RST · SYN · FIN	Window size
\multicolumn{2}{c	}{Checksum}	Urgent pointer

It contains fields as small as 1 bit, and as large as 32 bits. We shall use the following 20 byte TCP datagram header as an example: `00 26 bb 14 62 b7 cc 33 58 55 1e ed 08 00 45 00 03 78 f7 ac`.

The code in Figure 5.1, to print out pertinent information from the header, uses `getbit`, `getval`, and a yet-to-be-defined function `getval_32` to read the header of a TCP datagram and print a summary. The function `getval_32` returns up to 32 bits in an **Int32.t** (implementing `getval_32` is one of the questions at the end of the chapter). Here is the output for our example data:

```
Source port = 38
Destination = 47892
Sequence = 1656212531
Acknowledgement Number = 1481973485
Flags:
 Urgent = false
 Ack = false
 Push = false
 Reset = false
 Syn = false
 Fin = false
```

```
print_header : string → unit

let print_header filename =
  let ch = open_in_bin filename in
  let i = input_of_channel ch in
  let b = input_bits_of_input i in
    let src_port = getval b 16 in
    let dest_port = getval b 16 in
    let seq_number = getval_32 b 32 in
    let ack_number = getval_32 b 32 in
    let _ = getval b 4 in                       (* data offset *)
    let _ = getval b 6 in                       (* reserved *)
    let urgent = getbit b in
    let ack = getbit b in
    let push = getbit b in
    let reset = getbit b in
    let syn = getbit b in
    let fin = getbit b in
    let receive = getval b 16 in
    let checksum = getval b 16 in
    let urgent_pointer = getval b 16 in
      print_string "Source port = ";
      print_int src_port;
      print_string "\nDestination = ";
      print_int dest_port;
      print_string "\nSequence =";
      print_string (Int32.to_string seq_number);
      print_string "\nAcknowledgement Number = ";
      print_string (Int32.to_string ack_number);
      let print_bool b = print_string (string_of_bool b) in
        print_string "\nFlags:\n Urgent = "; print_bool urgent;
        print_string "\nAck = "; print_bool ack;
        print_string "\nPush = "; print_bool push;
        print_string "\nReset = "; print_bool reset;
        print_string "\nSyn = "; print_bool syn;
        print_string "\nFin = "; print_bool fin;
        print_string "Receive window size = ";
        print_int receive;
        print_string "\nChecksum = ";
        print_int checksum;
        print_string "\nUrgent pointer = ";
        print_int urgent_pointer;
        print_string "\n";
        close_in ch
```

Figure 5.1

```
Receive window size = 17664
Checksum = 888
Urgent pointer = 63404
```

Note we must use `open_in_bin` for binary data files in case the program is executed on Microsoft Windows, where text and binary files are considered different and read differently.

Output bit streams

The type for output bit streams is rather similar to that for input bit streams, but it must be used rather differently.

```
type output_bits =
  {output : output;
   mutable obyte : int;
   mutable obit : int}
```

Here, `output` is the underlying output. The current output byte which is being constructed bit-by-bit is `obyte`, and a number `obit` from 7 down to 0 to represent the current shift required to add a bit to the byte in the correct place. When it is time to move on to the next byte, `obit` is -1. We can build a fresh output_bits from an output:

```
output_bits_of_output : output → output_bits

let output_bits_of_output o =
  {output = o;
   obyte = 0;
   obit = 7}
```

The whole byte cannot be written to the underlying `output` until it has been completed, so we must have a `flush` function to be used when output is finished:

```
flush : output_bits → unit

let flush o =
  if o.obit < 7 then o.output.output_char (char_of_int o.obyte);
  o.obyte <- 0;
  o.obit <- 7
```

This doubles as our alignment function. We can now write `putbit`. For reasons we shall explain, it considers any non-zero input to be a **1** bit.

```
putbit : output_bits → int → unit

let rec putbit o b =
  if o.obit = (-1) then
    begin
      flush o;
      putbit o b
    end
  else
    begin
      if b <> 0 then o.obyte <- o.obyte lor (1 lsl o.obit);
      o.obit <- o.obit - 1
    end
```

To output a value of width up to 31, we can write a function `putval o v l` which, given an output_bits, value, and length in bits, calls `putbit` on each bit in turn:

```
putval : output_bits → int → int → unit

let putval o v l =
  for x = l - 1 downto 0 do
    putbit o (v land (1 lsl x))
  done
```

Now we can see why we allowed any non-zero integer to be considered a 1 bit – it avoids a test in `putval`. Now we have everything we need.

We can rebuild the datagram we took apart earlier using `putbit`, `putval`, and the yet-to-be-defined `putval_32` as shown in Figure 5.2. In the questions, you are asked to implement various specializations of some of our input and output functions on bit streams.

Chapter 5. Streams of Bits

```
output_header : string → unit

let output_header filename =
  let ch = open_out_bin filename in
  let o = output_of_channel ch in
  let bits = output_bits_of_output o in
    putval bits 38 16;
    putval bits 47892 16;
    putval_32 bits 1656212531l 32;
    putval_32 bits 1481973485l 32;
    putval bits 5 4;
    putval bits 0 6;
    putbit bits 0;
    putbit bits 0;
    putbit bits 0;
    putbit bits 0;
    putbit bits 0;
    putbit bits 0;
    putval bits 17664 16;
    putval bits 888 16;
    putval bits 63404 16;
    flush bits;
    close_out ch
```

Figure 5.2

Questions

1. Specialize the function `getval` so that writing 8 bits at a time when the input is aligned is optimized. Benchmark this function against the naive one.

2. Write the function `getval_32` which can get a value of type **Int32.t** in the same fashion as `getval`.

3. Specialize the function `putval` so that writing 8 bits at a time when the output is aligned is optimized. Benchmark this function against the naive one.

4. Write the function `putval_32` which can put a value of type **Int32.t** in the same fashion as `putval`.

5. We said that the output_bits type needed a `flush` operation. In fact, this is not always true – for outputs built with, for example, `output_of_bytes`, we could write the current byte every time a bit is written, seeking back one byte each time, only moving on when the byte is actually finished. Implement this.

Chapter 6

Compressing Data

Often we need to attempt to reduce the amount of space taken by some data, for storage or transmission. If data were arbitrary, it could not be compressed – to compress data we need to recognise and exploit patterns. However, most data is not arbitrary at all, but structured and containing repeated patterns. No compression scheme can guarantee to reduce the size of all inputs, but we would like to achieve good compression on typical data.

We will look at a simple byte-by-byte compression scheme, implementing it using our input and output data types so it can be applied to different kinds of inputs and outputs. Then, we will consider a more complex but efficient scheme for compressing data on a bit-by-bit basis.

A byte-by-byte compression scheme

The following extract from ISO-32000 (the PDF standard) defines a byte-by-byte compression scheme:

> The encoded data shall be a sequence of *runs*, where each run shall consist of a *length* byte followed by 1 to 128 bytes of data. If the *length* byte is in the range 0 to 127, the following *length* + 1 (1 to 128) bytes shall be copied literally during decompression. If the *length* is in the range 129 to 255, the following single byte shall be copied 257 - *length* (2 to 128) times during decompression. A *length* value of 128 shall denote EOD [end of data].

For example, consider the text "((5.000000, 4.583333), (4.500000,5.000000))", which can be represented in ASCII as the list of integers [40; 40; 53; 46; 48; 48; 48; 48; 48; 48; 44; 32; 52; 46; 53; 56; 51; 51; 51; 51; 41; 44; 32; 40; 52; 46; 53; 48; 48; 48; 48; 48; 44; 53; 46; 48; 48; 48; 48; 48; 48; 41; 41] of length 43. This will be compressed as shown in Figure 6.1. That is to say, as [255; 40; 1; 53; 46; 251; 48; 5; 44; 32; 52; 46; 53; 56; 253; 51; 6; 41; 44; 32; 40; 52; 46; 53; 252; 48; 2; 44; 53; 46; 251; 48; 255; 41; 128], of length 35. The maximum compression ratio achieved with this method (for long constant data) is 64:1. The worst case (alternating bytes) is 127:128 – a slight expansion.

Let us begin with two utility functions to allow us to convert between strings and lists of integers – this will make it easier to understand our examples when we evaluate them in OCaml's top level:

35

Input data	Type of run	Length	Output header	Output data
40 40	same	2	257 - 2 = 255	40
53 46	different	2	2 - 1 = 1	53 46
48 48 48 48 48 48	same	6	257 - 6 = 251	48
44 32 52 46 53 56	different	6	6 - 1 = 5	44 32 52 46 53 56
51 51 51 51	same	4	257 - 4 = 253	51
41 44 32 40 52 46 53	different	7	7 - 1 = 6	41 44 32 40 52 46 53
48 48 48 48 48	same	5	257 - 5 = 252	48
44 53 46	different	3	3 - 1 = 2	44 53 46
48 48 48 48 48 48	same	6	257 - 6 = 251	48
41 41	same	2	257 - 2 = 255	41
-	EOD	-	-	128

Figure 6.1

```
string_of_int_list : int list → string
int_list_of_string : string → int list

let string_of_int_list l =
  let b = Bytes.create (List.length l) in
    List.iteri (fun n x -> Bytes.set b n (char_of_int x)) l;
    Bytes.to_string b

let int_list_of_string s =
  let l = ref [] in
    for x = String.length s - 1 downto 0 do
      l := int_of_char s.[x] :: !l
    done;
    !l
```

Note the use of the Standard Library function `List.iteri` which is like `List.iter`, but it passes an additional integer to the function each time, representing the position in the list, starting at 0. Note also that we use **downto** in `int_list_of_string` to avoid a list reversal.

Now, we shall build a little abstraction to allow our compression and decompression functions to share a common basis. Our `compress` and `decompress` function will need to read from any input, and write to any output. However, for our little tests, we shall be reading from and writing to strings. Since we do not know the size of the compressed or decompressed output in advance, we cannot allocate an appropriately sized string. So, let us build an output from a **Buffer.t**. This way, we can write a function `process` which, given a compression or decompression function, creates a buffer, builds an output from it, calls the function to process the data, and then extracts the final string from the buffer.

Chapter 6. Compressing Data

```
output_of_buffer : Buffer.t → output
process : (input → output → unit) → string → string

let output_of_buffer b =
  {output_char = Buffer.add_char b;
   out_channel_length = fun () -> Buffer.length b}

let process f s =
  let b = Buffer.create (String.length s) in
    f (input_of_string s) (output_of_buffer b);
    Buffer.contents b
```

Now, given some suitable function `decompress`, say, we can call `process` giving the function and a string, and get a new string back.

Decompression in this scheme, as is often the case, is simpler than compression, so we shall address it first. The whole thing is wrapped in a loop which terminates only upon an exception. If the input data is well-formed, that exception will be EOD, which we have defined for this purpose. Inside the loop, we read a byte from the input. It is either in the range 0…127, in which case it is a "different" run, and we copy some bytes from input to output. Or, it is in the range 129…255, in which case it is a "same" run, and we output a number of copies of the next byte. Otherwise, the byte must have value 128, and we raise the EOD exception. The `decompress_string` function is as simple as we claimed it would be, because we wrote `process`.

```
decompress : input → output → unit
decompress_string : string → string

exception EOD

let decompress i o =
  try
    while true do
      match int_of_char (i.input_char ()) with
        x when x >= 0 && x <= 127 ->
          for p = 1 to x + 1 do o.output_char (i.input_char ()) done
      | x when x > 128 && x <= 255 ->
          let c = i.input_char () in
            for p = 1 to 257 - x do o.output_char c done
      | _ -> raise EOD
    done
  with
    EOD -> ()

let decompress_string = process decompress
```

For compression, we will first write functions to recognise a "same" run and a "different" run in the input, and then a main function which uses them as appropriate. The function `get_same` returns the first character, and an integer representing the number (one or more) of "same" characters starting with the first one. It leaves the input pointing at the last "same" character. If 128 same characters have been found, we must stop early. If we are at the end of input when the function is called, End_of_file is raised as usual.

```
get_same : input → char × int

let get_same i =
  let rec getcount ch c =
    if c = 128 then 128 else
      try
        if i.input_char () = ch
          then getcount ch (c + 1)
          else (rewind i; c)
      with
        End_of_file -> c
  in
    let ch = i.input_char () in (ch, getcount ch 1)
```

The get_different function is rather more awkward. It will return the non-empty list of "different" characters starting at the current position. We must stop as soon as we notice two like characters, rewinding twice and removing a character from our accumulator. So, for example, if we are reading "An Accumulation" we want to return ['A'; 'n'; ' '; 'A'] but we do not know this until we read the second 'c'. Again, we must stop after 128 differing characters. As before, End_of_file is raised if we are at the end of the input on the initial call.

```
get_different : input → char list

let get_different i =
  let rec getdiffinner a c =
    if c = 128 then List.rev a else
      try
        let ch' = i.input_char () in
          if ch' <> List.hd a
            then getdiffinner (ch' :: a) (c + 1)
            else (rewind i; rewind i; List.rev (List.tl a))
      with
        End_of_file -> List.rev a
  in
    getdiffinner [i.input_char ()] 1
```

The compression function is now relatively simple. We repeatedly call get_same. If it indicates a run of length one, we call get_different instead. In each case we write appropriate data. Then, on End_of_file, we write the EOD marker. The compress_string function is built just like decompress_string.

Chapter 6. Compressing Data

```ocaml
compress : input → output → unit

let compress i o =
  try
    while true do
      match get_same i with
        (_, 1) ->
          rewind i;
          let cs = get_different i in
            o.output_char (char_of_int (List.length cs - 1));
            List.iter o.output_char cs
      | (b, c) ->
          o.output_char (char_of_int (257 - c));
          o.output_char b
    done
  with
    End_of_file -> o.output_char (char_of_int 128)

let compress_string = process compress
```

Let us try with our sample data:

OCaml

```
# open Examples;;
# example;;
- : string = "((5.000000, 4.583333), (4.500000,5.000000))"

# int_list_of_string example;;
- : int list =
[40; 40; 53; 46; 48; 48; 48; 48; 48; 48; 44; 32; 52; 46; 53; 56; 51; 51; 51;
 51; 41; 44; 32; 40; 52; 46; 53; 48; 48; 48; 48; 48; 44; 53; 46; 48; 48; 48;
 48; 48; 48; 41; 41]

# let smaller = compress_string example;;
val smaller : string = "?(\0015.?0\005, 4.58?3\006), (4.5?0\002,5.?0?)\128"

# int_list_of_string smaller;;
- : int list =
[255; 40; 1; 53; 46; 251; 48; 5; 44; 32; 52; 46; 53; 56; 253; 51; 6; 41; 44;
 32; 40; 52; 46; 53; 252; 48; 2; 44; 53; 46; 251; 48; 255; 41; 128]

# decompress_string (compress_string example) = example;;
- : bool = true
```

A bit-by-bit compression scheme

Our previous method required whole bytes to be equal to one another to compress well. Now we consider compression bit-by-bit, but on the same principle – encoding the lengths of runs of data. We will build a compressor and decompressor for the CCITT Group 3 compression scheme. This is the basic scheme used by the fax machines since the 1970s, and for 1 bit-per-pixel TIFF files. It is also used in the PDF format, as we shall see later in the book. Here is our example data, an 80x21, one-bit-per-pixel image of a scanned word from printed paper:

We can put it into our source file using the characters 0 and 1 to ease readability. A string can run over several lines if a backslash is added at the end of each line. Spaces at the beginning of the next line are also skipped, so we can line it up nicely:

```
let input_data =
"00000000000000000000000000000000000000000000000000000000000000000000000000000000\
 00000000000000000000000000000000000000000000000000000000000000000000000001000000\
 00000000111111110000000000111111110000000000000000000000000000000000000111100000\
 00000011000000011100000001110000011100000000000000000000000000000000000011000000\
 00000110000000001110000011000000001100000000000000000000000000000000000011000000\
 00001110000000000111000111000000000000000000000000000000000000000000000011000000\
 00001100000000000111000110000000000000000000000000000000000000000000000011000000\
 00001100000000000110011100000000000000001110000000010011100011100000011000000\
 00011100000000000110011100000000000001111111000111111111011111100000001000000\
 00011100000000000111011000000000000010000110000011100011110001110000001000000\
 00011100000000000111011000000000000000110000011000001100001110000001000000\
 00011100000000000110011100000000000000110000011000001100001110000001000000\
 00001100000000000110011100000000000001110110000011000001100001110000001000000\
 00001110000000000110001100000000000001110001100000110000011000011000001000000\
 00001110000000000110000111000000000011000011000001100000110000011000011000000\
 00000111000000001100000111000000000011000011000001100000110000011000011100000\
 00000011100000011000000011100000001001000111000001100000110000011000111000000\
 00000011111111000000000011111111100011110111000111100011110000111001111100000\
 00000000011100000000000000111000000010000000000000000000000000000000000000000\
 00000000000000000000000000000000000000000000000000000000000000000000000000000\
 00000000000000000000000000000000000000000000000000000000000000000000000000000"
```

You can see that it consists of runs of 0 (white) and 1 (black) pixels, 80 to each line, with 21 lines.

Preliminaries

First, we had better define a function to convert the string of zeros and ones to a string containing the actual binary data. We can do this by building an output_bits with an output built from a buffer. Then, after flushing, we can use Buffer.contents to extract the data we have written.

Chapter 6. Compressing Data

```
packedstring_of_string : string → string

let packedstring_of_string s =
  let b = Buffer.create (String.length s / 8 + 1) in
  let o = output_bits_of_output (output_of_buffer b) in
    for x = 0 to String.length s - 1 do putbit o (s.[x] = '1') done;
    flush o;
    Buffer.contents b
```

Note that, since the string will always be a whole number of bytes (possibly padded with zeros by `flush`) we must remember the width and height of our image (80 and 21 here) and pass one or both of them to some of our other functions. For example, we can write a function to print one of these packed binary strings. This needs the width of the image to know when to print newlines:

```
print_packedstring : int → string → unit

let print_packedstring w s =
  let ibits = input_bits_of_input (input_of_string s) in
    try
      while true do
        for column = 1 to w do print_int (getbitint ibits) done;
        print_newline ()
      done
    with
      End_of_file -> ()
```

For simplicity here, we do not worry about padding at the end (in our example, since the width is 80, it will consist of whole bytes anyway).

Fax compression explained

We have said that the compression will proceed by encoding the lengths of the runs of zeros and ones in our data. How do we encode them? We need a set of binary sequences which can be distinguished from one another (i.e. no sequence can be a prefix of another sequence). In the case of fax compression, there are codes for run lengths 0 to 63, and different codes for white and black runs, as shown in Figure 6.2. Shorter codes are chosen for the more common cases, based on a statistical analysis of real documents.

Notice that no white symbol is a prefix of another white symbol, and no black symbol is a prefix of another black symbol. These codes for runs from 0 to 63 are called terminating codes. When a run is longer, we use one "make-up code", shown in Figure 6.3, followed by a terminating code. Thus, the longest run is of length 1728 + 63 = 1791.

The reason for distinguishing between white and black codes is to do with error correction in unreliable transport mechanisms (such as phone lines that fax machines operate over) – otherwise we could just have one set of codes and assume runs alternate. The reason for the existence of a zero-length run is that each line is defined to begin with a white run. If it is really black, a zero-length white run is output first. No run is longer than a line. As an example, let us compress the first three lines of our example data:

Run	White	Black	Run	White	Black	Run	White	Black
0	00110101	0000110111	22	0000011	00000110111	44	00101101	000001010100
1	000111	010	23	0000100	00000101000	45	00000100	000001010101
2	0111	11	24	0101000	00000010111	46	00000101	000001010110
3	1000	10	25	0101011	00000011000	47	00001010	000001010111
4	1011	011	26	0010011	000011001010	48	00001011	000001100100
5	1100	0011	27	0100100	000011001011	49	01010010	000001100101
6	1110	0010	28	0011000	000011001100	50	01010011	000001010010
7	1111	00011	29	00000010	000011001101	51	01010100	000001010011
8	10011	000101	30	00000011	000001101000	52	01010101	000000100100
9	10100	000100	31	00011010	000001101001	53	00100100	000000110111
10	00111	0000100	32	00011011	000001101010	54	00100101	000000111000
11	01000	0000101	33	00010010	000001101011	55	01011000	000000100111
12	001000	0000111	34	00010011	000011010010	56	01011001	000000101000
13	000011	00000100	35	00010100	000011010011	57	01011010	000001011000
14	110100	00000111	36	00010101	000011010100	58	01011011	000001011001
15	110101	000011000	37	00010110	000011010101	59	01001010	000000101011
16	101010	0000010111	38	00010111	000011010110	60	01001011	000000101100
17	101011	0000011000	39	00101000	000011010111	61	00110010	000001011010
18	0100111	0000001000	40	00101001	000001101100	62	00110011	000001100110
19	0001100	00001100111	41	00101010	000001101101	63	00110100	000001100111
20	0001000	00001101000	42	00101011	000011011010	(make up codes required		
21	0010111	00001101100	43	00101100	000011011011	for longer runs)		

Figure 6.2

Chapter 6. Compressing Data

Run	White	Black	Run	White	Black
64	11011	0000001111	960	011010100	0000001110011
128	10010	000011001000	1024	011010101	0000001110100
192	010111	000011001001	1088	011010110	0000001110101
256	0110111	000001011011	1152	011010111	0000001110110
320	00110110	000000110011	1216	011011000	0000001110111
384	00110111	000000110100	1280	011011001	0000001010010
448	01100100	000000110101	1344	011011010	0000001010011
512	01100101	0000001101100	1408	011011011	0000001010100
576	01101000	0000001101101	1472	010011000	0000001010101
640	01100111	0000001001010	1536	010011001	0000001011010
704	011001100	0000001001011	1600	010011010	0000001011011
768	0 11001101	0000001001100	1664	011000	0000001100100
832	011010010	0000001001101	1728	010011011	0000001100101
896	011010011	0000001110010			

Figure 6.3

```
0000000000000000000000000000000000000000000000000000000000000000000000000000000000
0000000000000000000000000000000000000000000000000000000000000000000000000001000000
0000000011111111000000000001111111100000000000000000000000000000000000000111100000
```

We have the following:

Length	Colour	Code
80	White	11011 + 101010
73	White	11011 + 10100
1	Black	010
6	White	1110
8	White	1011
8	Black	000101
11	White	01000
9	Black	000100
35	White	00010100
4	Black	011
5	White	1100

We have reduced the data from 240 bits to 64 bits, a reduction of about three quarters.

Compressing fax data

First, we need to encode the terminating and make-up codes. We will use arrays for direct indexing, but lists for each element, since we do not need random access to each bit. This is shown in Figure 6.4. Now, we can write a function which, given a length of run and a colour, gives the appropriate code as a list of bits:

```
code : bool → int → int list

let rec code isblack length =
  if length > 1791 || length < 0 then
    raise (Invalid_argument "code: bad length")
  else
    if length > 64 then
      let m =
        if isblack
          then black_make_up_codes.(length / 64 - 1)
          else white_make_up_codes.(length / 64 - 1)
      in
        m @ code isblack (length mod 64)
    else
      if isblack
        then black_terminating_codes.(length)
        else white_terminating_codes.(length)
```

Now, a function which, given the current colour, an input_bits, the current number of like bits read, and the width of the image, returns a pair of the number of like bits, and the colour (`peekbit` is a generally useful function – it returns one bit without advancing):

```
peekbit : input_bits → int
read_up_to : int → input_bits → int → int → int × int

let peekbit b =
  if b.bit = 0 then
    begin
      let byte = int_of_char (b.input.input_char ()) in
        rewind b.input;
        byte land 128 > 0
    end
  else
    b.byte land b.bit > 0

let rec read_up_to v i n w =
  if n >= w then (n, v) else
    if peekbit i = v
      then (ignore (getbit i); read_up_to v i (n + 1) w)
      else (n, v)
```

Chapter 6. Compressing Data

```
white_terminating_codes : int list array
black_terminating_codes : int list array
white_make_up_codes : int list array
black_make_up_codes : int list array

let white_terminating_codes =
  [|[0; 0; 1; 1; 0; 1; 0; 1];
    [0; 0; 0; 1; 1; 1];
    [0; 1; 1; 1];
    [1; 0; 0; 0];
    [1; 0; 1; 1];
    [1; 1; 0; 0];                               and so on...

let black_terminating_codes =
  [|[0; 0; 0; 1; 1; 0; 1; 1; 1];
    [0; 1; 0];
    [1; 1];
    [1; 0];
    [0; 1; 1];
    [0; 0; 1; 1];                               and so on...

let white_make_up_codes =
  [|[1; 1; 0; 1; 1];
    [1; 0; 0; 1; 0];
    [0; 1; 0; 1; 1; 1];
    [0; 1; 1; 0; 1; 1; 1];
    [0; 0; 1; 1; 0; 1; 1; 0];
    [0; 0; 1; 1; 0; 1; 1; 1];                   and so on...

let black_make_up_codes =
  [|[0; 0; 0; 0; 0; 1; 1; 1; 1];
    [0; 0; 0; 0; 1; 1; 0; 0; 1; 0; 0];
    [0; 0; 0; 0; 1; 1; 0; 0; 1; 0; 1];
    [0; 0; 0; 0; 0; 1; 0; 1; 1; 0; 1; 1];
    [0; 0; 0; 0; 0; 0; 1; 1; 0; 0; 1; 1];
    [0; 0; 0; 0; 0; 0; 1; 1; 0; 1; 0; 0];       and so on...
```

Figure 6.4

For example, the first call to read_up_to will calculate (80, 0). Now we can write the main function. Given an input_bits and output_bits, and the width and height of the image, for each line we check if a zero-width white run needs to be added, and then call encode_fax_line.

```
encode_fax : input_bits → output_bits → int → int → unit

let encode_fax i o w h =
  let rec encode_fax_line i o w =
    if w > 0 then
      let n, isblack = read_up_to (peekbit i) i 0 w in
        List.iter (putbitint o) (code isblack n);
        encode_fax_line i o (w - n)
  in
    for x = 1 to h do
      if peekbit i then List.iter (putbitint o) (code false 0);
      encode_fax_line i o w
    done
```

Now we can write a function process, just like we did in the byte-by-byte example, but for input_bits and output_bits. We must be sure to flush the output. The main compress_string_ccitt function is then simple:

```
process : (input_bits → output_bits → int → int → unit) →
          string → int → int → string
compress_string_ccitt : (int → int → unit) → string → int → int → string

let process f s w h =
  let b = Buffer.create (String.length s) in
  let ibits = input_bits_of_input (input_of_string s) in
  let obits = output_bits_of_output (output_of_buffer b) in
    f ibits obits w h;
    flush obits;
    Buffer.contents b

let compress_string_ccitt = process encode_fax
```

For our full input data, the input string is $80 \times 21 = 1680$ bits long, and the compressed string is 960 bits long, a compression ratio of 7:4.

Decompressing fax data

For decompression, we will write two functions for reading white and black codes. It is easiest to directly encode the decision tree:

```
read_white_code : input_bits -> int
read_black_code : input_bits -> int

let rec read_white_code i =
  let a = getbitint i in
  let b = getbitint i in
  let c = getbitint i in
  let d = getbitint i in
    match a, b, c, d with
      0, 1, 1, 1 -> 2
    | 1, 0, 0, 0 -> 3
    | 1, 0, 1, 1 -> 4
    | 1, 1, 0, 0 -> 5
    | 1, 1, 1, 0 -> 6
    | 1, 1, 1, 1 -> 7
    | _ ->
  let e = getbitint i in
    match a, b, c, d, e with
      1, 0, 0, 1, 1 -> 8
    | 1, 0, 1, 0, 0 -> 9
    | 0, 0, 1, 1, 1 -> 10
    | 0, 1, 0, 0, 0 -> 11
    | 1, 1, 0, 1, 1 -> 64 + read_white_code i
    | 1, 0, 0, 1, 0 -> 128 + read_white_code i
    | _ ->
  let f = getbitint i in
    match a, b, c, d, e, f with
      0, 0, 0, 1, 1, 1 -> 1                          and so on...

let rec read_black_code i =
  let a = getbitint i in
  let b = getbitint i in
    match a, b with
      1, 1 -> 2
    | 1, 0 -> 3
    | _ ->
  let c = getbitint i in
    match a, b, c with
      0, 1, 0 -> 1
    | 0, 1, 1 -> 4
    | _ ->
  let d = getbitint i in
  match a, b, c, d with
    0, 0, 1, 1 -> 5                                  and so on...
```

Now, decoding is relatively simple. We decode runs for each line, until the width is all used up, and do this for each line. We read white and black codes alternately – each line begins on white. We can use process again:

```
decode_fax : input_bits → output_bits → int → int → unit
decompress_string_ccitt : (int → int → unit) → string → int → int → string

let decode_fax i o w h =
  let lines = ref h in
  let pixels = ref w in
  let iswhite = ref true in
    while !lines > 0 do
      while !pixels > 0 do
        let n =
          (if !iswhite then read_white_code else read_black_code) i
        in
          for x = 1 to n do
            putbitint o (if !iswhite then 0 else 1)
          done;
          pixels := !pixels - n;
          iswhite := not !iswhite
      done;
      iswhite := true;
      pixels := w;
      lines := !lines - 1
    done

let decompress_string_ccitt = process decode_fax
```

We can verify our code by evaluating s = decompress_string_ccitt (compress_string_ccitt s) for our example data.

Questions

1. How much complexity did using the input and output types add to `compress` and `decompress` in our byte-by-byte example? Rewrite the functions so they just operate over lists of integers, in functional style, and compare the two.

2. Replace our manual tree of codes with a tree automatically generated from the lists of codes used for compression. The tree will have no data at its branches (since no code is a prefix of another), and will have data at only some of its leaves. Define a suitable data type first.

3. What happens if we compress our data as a single line of 1680 bits instead of 21 lines of 80? What happens if we try to compress already-compressed data?

4. Write a function which, given input data, will calculate a histogram of the frequencies of different runs of white and black. This could be used to build custom codes for each image, improving compression.

Chapter 7

Labelled and Optional Arguments

OCaml allows us to label some or all of the arguments to a function, so as to provide a little documentation, to prevent us from accidently swapping two arguments which have the same type, and to allow partial application of arguments more flexibly. Consider a function to fill in part of an array with an element:

```
fill   : α array → int → int → α → unit
filled : unit → string array

let fill a s l v =
  for x = s to s + l - 1 do a.(x) <- v done

let filled () =
  let a = Array.make 100 "x" in
    fill a 20 40 "y";
    a
```

The `fill` function takes four arguments: the array itself, the start position, length of the fill and the element to use to fill. However, since the start and length are both integers, it is easy to get them the wrong way round. This can be remedied by giving those two arguments *labels*. A label is introduced by a tilde, followed by the label name, a colon and the argument name itself. Consider the functions `fill` and `filled` below. As you can see, we have defined `fill` with labels, which appear in the type as well. In the first `filled` function, we call the `fill` function, citing the labels and giving immediate integers. In the second, we show that it works with other names (as it does, indeed, for any expression). In the third, we show that the labelled arguments may be permuted and rearranged with regard to the other arguments (unlabelled arguments must remain in the correct order relative to one another).

```
fill : α array → start:int → length:int → α → unit
filled : unit → string array

let fill a ~start:s ~length:l v =
  for x = s to s + l - 1 do a.(x) <- v done

let filled () =
  let a = Array.make 100 "x" in
    fill a ~start:20 ~length:40 "y";
    a

let filled () =
  let a = Array.make 100 "x" in
    let st = 20 in
      let ln = 40 in
        fill a ~start:st ~length:ln "y";
        a

let filled () =
  let a = Array.make 100 "x" in
    fill a "y" ~length:20 ~start:40;
    a
```

Another change we can make is to use the label for the name of the argument inside the function too. This simplifies the syntax: we can just write ~label.

```
fill : α array → start:int → length:int → α → unit
filled : unit → string array

let fill a ~start ~length v =
  for x = start to start + length - 1 do a.(x) <- v done

let filled () =
  let a = Array.make 100 "x" in
    let start = 20 in
      let length = 40 in
        fill a ~start ~length "y";
        a
```

You can see that in filled, this "punning" works equally well when calling the function, if we happen to have values with the same names. These two facilities need not be used together, of course.

Labels with partial application

Another common use of labelled arguments is to give flexibility when using partial application. Consider the following function:

Chapter 7. Labelled and Optional Arguments

```
let divide x y = x / y
```

We can use partial application to write the function which divides ten thousand by each number in a list:

```
let f = divide 10000 in [f 100; f 50; f 20]
```

This yields `[100; 200; 500]`. But we cannot re-use `divide` to write the function which divides each number in a list by ten – this would involve partially applying the second argument `y` first. The design of the `divide` function has baked in which argument may be partially applied (OCaml lets us partially apply any prefix of the arguments – the first, first and second, first, second and third etc.) For example, we can apply the same function to many lists, using a partially applied `List.map` but we cannot apply many functions to a single list by providing the list to `List.map` instead. In our example, we can label the arguments to our divide function:

```
let divide ~x ~y = x / y
```

The type of the function reflects this:

OCaml
```
# let divide ~x ~y = x / y;;
val divide : x:int -> y:int -> int = <fun>
```

Now we may apply the arguments in either order:

OCaml
```
# let f = divide ~x:10000 in [f 100; f 50; f 20];;
- : int list = [100; 200; 500]
# let f = divide ~y:10000 in [f 100000; f 10000; f 1000];;
- : int list = [10; 1; 0]
```

We can in fact, omit the labels if we are applying arguments in order:

OCaml
```
# let f = divide 10000 in [f 100; f 50; f 20];;
- : int list = [100; 200; 500]
```

Optional arguments

OCaml also allows us to make a labelled argument optional – that is to say, we need not supply it at all. The function which is called without one or more of its arguments can decide what to do. Consider this simple function `split` which returns a list of singleton lists from an input list, for example returning `[[1]; [2]; [3]]` for the input list `[1; 2; 3]`:

```
split : α list → α list list

let rec split l =
  match l with
    [] -> []
  | h::t -> [h] :: split t
```

We would like to extend the function to produce sub-lists of a given size, other than the default of 1. We can add a labelled argument and adapt the function, using `take` (which takes a given number of items from the start of a list) and `drop` (which drops a given number of items from the start of a list) from the Util module described on page xiii:

```
split : chunksize:int → α list → α list list

let rec split ~chunksize l =
  try
    Util.take l chunksize ::
    split ~chunksize (Util.drop l chunksize)
  with
    _ -> match l with [] -> [] | _ -> [l]         last, partial, chunk
```

There are two problems, though. Existing code using the function will not compile, and we must always specify the `chunksize` argument, even when it will be 1. This can be remedied by using an *optional* labelled argument, introduced with a question mark instead of a tilde, and given a default value:

```
split : ?chunksize:int → α list → α list list

let rec split ?(chunksize = 1) l =
  try
    Util.take l chunksize ::
    split ~chunksize (Util.drop l chunksize)
  with
    _ -> match l with [] -> [] | _ -> [l]         last, partial, chunk
```

Notice the question mark appears also in the type. Notice also that in the recursive call to `split` we can write `~chunksize` instead of `~chunksize:chunksize` as usual. Now our `split` function can be called with or without this optional argument:

Chapter 7. Labelled and Optional Arguments

OCaml

```
# split [1; 2; 3];;
- : int list list = [[1]; [2]; [3]]
# split ~chunksize:3 [1; 2; 3; 4; 5; 6; 7];;
- : int list list = [[1; 2; 3]; [4; 5; 6]; [7]]
```

In fact, if we do not give a default value to the optional argument in the definition of split, we have access to its actual implementation – as a value of the **option** type, either None or Some, and we can match on it:

```
split : ?chunksize:int → α list → α list list

let rec split ?chunksize l =
  let ch =
    match chunksize with None -> 1 | Some x -> x
  in
    try
      Util.take l ch :: split ~chunksize:ch (Util.drop l ch)
    with
      _ -> match l with [] -> [] | _ -> [l]
```

This is primarily useful when there are several optional arguments.

Labels in the Standard Library

The Standard Library contains three labelled versions of other modules: **ListLabels**, **ArrayLabels** and **StringLabels**. For example, we can write:

OCaml

```
# ListLabels.map ~f:(fun x -> x * 2) [1; 2; 3];;
- : int list = [2; 4; 6]
```

If we wish to use the labelled modules by default, the module **StdLabels** contains these labelled modules under their original names so, by writing "open StdLabels", List.map, Array.blit etc. will now be labelled:

OCaml

```
# open StdLabels;;
# List.map ~f:(fun x -> x * 2) [1; 2; 3];;
- : int list = [2; 4; 6]
```

These modules do not label all arguments. Typically they just do so for arguments which are functions, and when there are multiple arguments of the same type which may be confused. For example, ArrayLabels.sub of type α **array** → pos:**int** → len:**int** → α **array** introduces labels to disambiguate the position and length arguments, but does not label in the input array.

Questions

1. The function `ArrayLabels.make` is not labelled, having type **int** $\to \alpha \to \alpha$ **array**. When might this cause confusion? Write a labelled version to correct this problem.

2. When we wrote our `fill` function with labelled arguments, we wanted to prevent someone mistakenly swapping the start and length values. Can you find a way to do this without labelled or optional arguments?

3. Build labelled versions of functions from the **Buffer** module, choosing which functions and arguments to label as appropriate.

4. Frequently we use an accumulator to make a function tail-recursive, wrapping it up in another function to give the initial value of the accumulator. For example, we might write:

   ```
   map_inner : α list → (α → β) → α list → β list
   map : (α → β) → α list → β list

   let rec map_inner a f l =
     match l with
       [] -> List.rev a
     | h::t -> map_inner (f h :: a) f t

   let map f l = map_inner [] f l
   ```

   Use an optional argument to express this as a single function.

Chapter 8

Formatted Printing

OCaml provides facilities for what is called formatted printing. Consider the following function, culled from Chapter 3:

```
string_of_point : point → string

let string_of_point p =
  p.label
  ^ " = ("
  ^ string_of_float p.x
  ^ ", "
  ^ string_of_float p.y
  ^ ")"
```

Using the function `sprintf` ("**f**ormatted **print**ing to a **s**tring") from the Standard Library module **Printf** we can build this string more easily:

```
string_of_point : point → string

let string_of_point p =
  Printf.sprintf "%s = (%f, %f)" p.label p.x p.y
```

In this example, the *format string* is "`%s = (%f, %f)`". The *conversion specifications* `%s` and `%f` denote places for a string and the decimal representation of a floating-point number respectively to be substituted into the string. Other characters are simply reproduced from the format string to the output string. We have avoided the inefficient, repeated use of the `^` operator for string concatenation, and our new example is both shorter and easier to read. Here is a subset of the many conversion specifications available:

Conversion specification	Description
%i	integer in decimal representation
%x	integer in hexadecimal, lower case
%X	integer in hexadecimal, upper case
%s	string
%f	floating-point number
%B	boolean
%%	percent character
%!	flush the output

The `sprintf` function knows how to match up the conversion specification with the arguments following the format specification at compile time, so run-time errors are avoided:

OCaml

```
# Printf.sprintf "%s = (%f, %f)" "A" 40 65.8;;
Error: This expression has type int but an expression was expected of type
       float
```

Indeed, even if we use partial application, the type of the resulting function will be calculated:

OCaml

```
# let f = Printf.sprintf "%s = (%f, %f)" "A" 2.45;;
val f : float -> string = <fun>
```

You might be able to guess that there is a little magic going on here – we could not write `sprintf` ourselves, for example. We can see the rather complicated type of the `sprintf` function, used for its internal implementation:

OCaml

```
# Printf.sprintf;;
- : ('a, unit, string) format -> 'a = <fun>
```

For printing numbers, there are some additional pieces of information which can be provided. The format of a conversion specifier is in fact:

%⟨flags⟩⟨width⟩⟨.precision⟩type

Fields enclosed in angle brackets are optional. So far, we have only used the % character and the *type* field. The *width* field defines the width of the representation of the number, and can be used to line things up in columns, here of width six:

Chapter 8. Formatted Printing

```
data : (int × int × int) list
print_header : unit → unit
print_line : int → int → int → unit
print_nums : (int × int × int) list → unit

let data =
  [(1, 6, 5);
   (2, 18, 4);
   (3, 31, 12);
   (4, 16, 2)]

let print_header () =
  Printf.printf "A      | B      | C      \n";
  Printf.printf "------+-------+-------\n"

let print_line a b c =
  Printf.printf "%6i| %6i| %6i\n" a b c

let print_nums nums =
  print_header ();
  List.iter (fun (a, b, c) -> print_line a b c) nums
```

This will result in the following output from `print_nums data`:

```
A      | B      | C
------+-------+-------
    1|      6|      5
    2|     18|      4
    3|     31|     12
    4|     16|      2
```

Here are some possible values of the *flags* field:

Flag	Description
-	left-justify within width (the default is to right-justify)
0	pad number within width with zeros instead of spaces
+	prefix positive number with +

The optional *precision* field specifies the number of digits after the decimal point. For example, let us print some integers and floating-point numbers in columns with differing flags and precisions:

```
data : (int × float × float) list
print_header : unit → unit
print_line : int → float → float → unit
print_nums : (int × float × float) list → unit

let data =
  [(1, 35.54263, 39.42312);
   (2, 12.31341, 23.24123);
   (3, 13.53342, 23.21457);
   (4, 57.74572, 126.74554)]

let print_header () =
  Printf.printf "A      | B      | C     \n";
  Printf.printf "------+-------+-------\n"

let print_line a b c =
  Printf.printf "%06i| %-6.2f| %-6.2f\n" a b c

let print_nums nums =
  print_header ();
  List.iter (fun (a, b, c) -> print_line a b c) nums
```

This will result in the following output from `print_nums data`:

```
A      | B      | C
------+-------+-------
000001| 35.54  | 39.42
000002| 12.31  | 23.24
000003| 13.53  | 24.21
000004| 57.75  | 126.75
```

Printing to other places

Of course, once we have calculated a string using `sprintf`, we can do with it what we may – however, for convenience and efficiency, the **Printf** module provides several other functions:

Function	Description
`printf`	writes to standard output (`printf format arg1...argN`)
`eprintf`	writes to standard error (`eprintf format arg1...argN`)
`bprintf`	writes to a given **Buffer.t** (`bprintf buffer format arg1...argN`)
`fprintf`	writes to a given out_channel (`fprintf channel format arg1...argN`)

These all return **unit**. For example, to write a point to standard output, using the `%!` conversion specification to flush each time so screen update is immediate:

```
print_point : point → unit

let print_point p =
  Printf.printf "%s = (%f, %f)%!" p.label p.x p.y
```

It might be argued, though, that it is better to keep `string_of_point` as the basic function, so it can be reused in other situations, writing the generated string to the screen from the calling function instead.

Questions

1. Given a list of pairs of integers such as [(1, 2); (5, 6); (6, 6); (7, 5)], write a function to return a string representation such as "(1, 2) --> (5, 6) --> (6, 6) --> (7, 5) --> (1, 2)".

2. Write a function which, given a string, returns another string which represents the first using hexadecimal numbers. For example, the input string `Hello` should yield the output `48656c6c6f` since 'H' has ASCII code `0x48` and so on.

3. Why does the following code cause a type error?

    ```
    # let mkstring () = "string";;
    val mkstring : unit -> string = <fun>
    # Printf.printf (mkstring ());
      ;;
    Error: This expression has type string but an expression was expected of type
             ('a, out_channel, unit) format =
                 ('a, out_channel, unit, unit, unit, unit) format6
    ```

    What can be done to fix it?

4. Use the * syntax described in the **Printf** module documentation to write a function which can print a table of integers to a given width. For example, given width 10, we might see:

    ```
    (         1)
    (        23)
    (     33241)
    (         0)
    ```

Chapter 9

Searching for Things

How do we look for a sequence in another, longer sequence? Suppose we want to write a function search_list which, given the list p (the *pattern*) to search for in the list l determines if it exists (i.e. if it is a sub-list). For example, the list [1; 2] is found in [2; 1; 2; 2] but not in [2; 1; 1]. A list p is defined to be a sub-list of a list l if there exist lists x and y such that l = x @ p @ y. One, two, three, or all four of x, p, y, l can be the empty list, of course. So, for example, [] is a sub-list of [1; 2; 3] and of []. A list p is a sub-list of l if:

- The length of p is less than or equal to the length of l and *either*
- The sub-list p is found at the beginning of l, *or*
- The list p is a sub-list of the tail of l

We can write this out easily, using the take and drop functions from our Util module, described on page xiii:

```
search_list : α list → α list → bool

let rec search_list p l =
    List.length p <= List.length l
  &&
    (Util.take l (List.length p) = p || search_list p (List.tl l))
```

(Recall that the || operator does not evaluate its right hand side if the left hand side evaluates to true, so this function will exit as soon as it finds a match.) We might be worried about the call List.tl failing, but if l is empty, the pattern must be empty from the first test, and so the condition with Util.take would have succeeded already. You can see that there are two inefficiencies here, the use of List.length on p and l each time around, and the explicit building of the list to check the pattern against with Util.take. Let us remove the first one:

```
search_list_inner : α list → int → α list → int → bool
search_list : α list → α list → bool

let rec search_list_inner p len_p l len_l =
    len_p <= len_l
  &&
    (Util.take l len_p = p ||
      search_list_inner p len_p (List.tl l) (len_l - 1))

let search_list p l =
  search_list_inner p (List.length p) l (List.length l)
```

Now, `List.length` is called only at the beginning. We can also remove `Util.take` to avoid the construction of intermediate lists, by writing an explicit function to test the pattern against the first `len_p` items in the lists:

```
equal : α list → int → α list → bool
search_list_inner : α list → int → α list → int → bool
search_list : α list → α list → bool

let rec equal l len p =
    len = 0
  ||
    List.hd l = List.hd p && equal (List.tl l) (len - 1) (List.tl p)

let rec search_list_inner p len_p l len_l =
    len_p <= len_l
  &&
    (equal l len_p p ||
      search_list_inner p len_p (List.tl l) (len_l - 1))

let search_list p l =
  search_list_inner p (List.length p) l (List.length l)
```

This is now about as efficient as our simple approach can get.

Searching in strings

For practical applications, we shall often need to search within strings, or other such random-access structures. Our first list version generalizes easily:

Chapter 9. Searching for Things

```
search : string → string → bool

let rec search p s =
    String.length p <= String.length s
  &&
    (String.sub s 0 (String.length p) = p ||
     search p (String.sub s 1 (String.length s - 1)))
```

This time, there is no problem with `String.length` since, unlike `List.length`, it runs in constant time. We do have the overhead of the first `String.sub`, analogous to the `Util.take` in the list version. The second `String.sub` is also a problem since, unlike `List.tl`, it creates a new string.

To solve this, we can define an auxiliary function `at` which, given pattern p, string s and the length l to test, together with the position in the pattern pp and in the main string sp, tests for equality. This is similar to `equal` in our lists example.

```
at : string → int → string → int → int → bool
search' : int → string → string → bool
search : string → string → bool

let rec at p pp s sp l =
  l = 0 || p.[pp] = s.[sp] && at p (pp + 1) s (sp + 1) (l - 1)

let rec search' n p s =
    String.length p <= String.length s - n
  &&
    (at p 0 s n (String.length p) || search' (n + 1) p s)

let search = search' 0
```

The `search'` function itself has a counter for how far along the main string it is. We initialize this to zero in `search`.

More flexible searches

We can make our searching function more interesting by allowing the use of some special characters. We shall introduce only these simple constructs:

- A ? character matches zero or one instances of the following character. For example, the pattern ?abc matches abc, bc, and dbc;
- A * character matches zero or more instances of the following character. So, the pattern *abc matches bc, abc, and aaabc;
- A + character matches one or more instances of the following character. For example, the pattern +abc matches abc and aaabc but not bc or dbc.

Let us add the ? character to begin with. First, we must alter our `search'` function's terminating condition – we can no longer just finish when the pattern is longer than the remaining part of the string – the length of the pattern and the length of the characters matching that pattern are no longer always equal. We now continue only when the position n is less than the length of the string, or it is equal to the length of the string and that length is zero (the latter case is required so that the pattern ?a matches the empty string).

```
search' : int → string → string → bool
search  : string → string → bool

let rec search' n p s =
  (n < String.length s || n = 0 && String.length s = 0) &&
  (at p 0 s n || search' (n + 1) p s)

let search = search' 0
```

Now we can alter the at function itself. We have an initial terminating condition – if the pattern has been used up entirely, we must have matched it. Otherwise, we match on the next character in the pattern, to see if the next part of the pattern matches and, if it does, calculate jump_p (the amount to move forward in the pattern) and jump_s (the amount to move forward in the string).

```
at : string → int → string → int → bool

let rec at p pp s sp =
  pp > String.length p - 1 ||                           whole pattern used – match
  match
    match p.[pp] with
    | '?' ->
        if pp + 1 > String.length p - 1 then None          end pattern
        else if sp > String.length s - 1 then Some (2, 0)  end string
        else if p.[pp + 1] = s.[sp] then Some (2, 1)       the character
        else Some (2, 0)                                   any other character
    | c ->
        if sp < String.length s && c = s.[sp] then
          Some (1, 1)
        else
          None
  with
    None -> false                                       match failure – stop
  | Some (jump_p, jump_s) ->
      at p (pp + jump_p) s (sp + jump_s)                match success – continue
```

Note the behaviour of the ? case carefully, with regard to its specification – this kind of matching code can be rather subtle. To deal with * we must have a way of matching zero or more instances of a character, moving as far along the string as possible. The function swallow_all below, given a character ch, a string p and a position sp, returns the number of characters which match ch starting at sp. We can then add a match case for the * specifier, as shown in Figure 9.1.

The + character can be added with swallow_all too, but we must check that there is at least one matching character. Figure 9.2 shows the whole program in one place.

```
swallow_all : char → string → int → int
at : string → int → string → int → bool

let swallow_all ch s sp =
  let x = ref sp in
    while !x < String.length s && s.[!x] = ch do x := !x + 1 done;
    !x - sp

let rec at p pp s sp =
  pp > String.length p - 1 ||              whole pattern used – match
  match
    match p.[pp] with
    | '?' ->
        if pp + 1 > String.length p - 1 then None            end pattern
        else if sp > String.length s - 1 then Some (2, 0)     end string
        else if p.[pp + 1] = s.[sp] then Some (2, 1)        the character
        else Some (2, 0)                              any other character
    | '*' ->
        if pp + 1 > String.length p - 1 then None else        end pattern
          Some (2, swallow_all p.[pp + 1] s sp)          read zero or more
        else None                                           did not match
    | c ->
        if sp < String.length s && c = s.[sp] then
          Some (1, 1)
        else
          None
  with
    None -> false                                  match failure – stop
  | Some (jump_p, jump_s) ->
      at p (pp + jump_p) s (sp + jump_s)         match success – continue
```

Figure 9.1

```
swallow_all : char → string → int → int
at : string → int → string → int → bool
search' : int → string → string → bool
search : string → string → bool

let swallow_all ch s sp =
  let x = ref sp in
    while !x < String.length s && s.[!x] = ch do x := !x + 1 done;
    !x - sp

let rec at p pp s sp =
  pp > String.length p - 1 ||                      whole pattern used – match
  match
    match p.[pp] with
    | '?' ->
        if pp + 1 > String.length p - 1 then None           end pattern
        else if sp > String.length s - 1 then Some (2, 0)   end string
        else if p.[pp + 1] = s.[sp] then Some (2, 1)        the character
        else Some (2, 0)                                    any other character
    | '*' ->
        if pp + 1 > String.length p - 1 then None else      end pattern
          Some (2, swallow_all p.[pp + 1] s sp)             read zero or more
    | '+' ->
        if pp + 1 > String.length p - 1 then None           end pattern
        else if sp > String.length s - 1 then None          end string
        else if p.[pp + 1] = s.[sp] then
          Some (2, swallow_all p.[pp + 1] s sp)             read one or more
        else None                                           did not match
    | c ->
        if sp < String.length s && c = s.[sp] then
          Some (1, 1)
        else
          None
  with
    None -> false                                  match failure – stop
  | Some (jump_p, jump_s) ->
      at p (pp + jump_p) s (sp + jump_s)           match success – continue

let rec search' n ss s =
  (n < String.length s || n = 0 && String.length s = 0) &&
  (at ss 0 s n || search' (n + 1) ss s)

let search = search' 0
```

Figure 9.2

Questions

1. Write a function to return the number of matches of one string in another a) when all matches are considered and b) when only non-overlapping matches are considered.

2. Write functions which return the position and length of the longest prefix of a string in another. That is to say, the longest initial part of the pattern which matches anywhere in the string.

3. Compare the speed of the first two versions of `search` given in this chapter.

4. Add the special symbol \ to our final search program. It indicates that the following symbol is not a special symbol, but a normal character. Note that, we must write '\\' for that character in OCaml code.

5. Add a labelled argument of type **bool** whose value, when true, indicates a case-insensitive search.

Chapter 10

Finding Permutations

How can we calculate the $n!$ permutations of a given list of length n? For example, given the list [1; 2; 3] we should like to find [[1; 2; 3]; [2; 1; 3]; [2; 3; 1]; [1; 3; 2]; [3; 1; 2]; [3; 2; 1]] or similar (we are not concerned with the order of the list of permutations). So, we require a function of type α list $\rightarrow \alpha$ list list.

Sometimes it is useful with a hard problem like this to simply start writing, working out what gaps there are, and then filling them in. The base case for our perms function is trivial: there is one permutation of the empty list, namely the empty list itself:

```
perms : α list → α list list

let perms p =
  match p with
    [] -> [[]]
```

For the main case, let us try the most simple decomposition. We calculate the permutations of the tail for free with recursion, and then combine the result in some way with the head:

```
perms : α list → α list list

let rec perms p =
  match p with
    [] -> [[]]
  | h::t -> combine h (perms t)
```

Here, combine is a function we have yet to concoct. It must take a list of permutations, such as [[3; 2]; [2; 3]] and a single element, such as 1, and produce [[1; 2; 3]; [2; 1; 3]; [2; 3; 1]; [1; 3; 2]; [3; 1; 2]; [3; 2; 1]]. The elements of this list can be produced by placing 1 in each possible place in each list in [[3; 2]; [2; 3]]. So first, we will reduce the problem by using List.map with an as-yet-unwritten function interleave, combining the results with List.concat:

```
combine : α → α list list → α list
perms : α list → α list list

let combine x ps =
  List.concat (List.map (interleave x) ps)

let rec perms p =
  match p with
    [] -> [[]]
  | h::t -> combine h (perms t)
```

Now, we just need to build the function `interleave` which takes an item, such as 1 and a list such as [2; 3] and builds the list [[1; 2; 3]; [2; 1; 3]; [2; 3; 1]] by placing the item at each possible position in the list.

```
interleave : α → α list → α list → α list list

let rec interleave e seen l =
  match l with
    [] -> [seen @ [e]]
  | x::xs -> (seen @ e :: x :: xs) :: interleave e (seen @ [x]) xs
```

This function maintains a list of the elements already seen (which is initially empty), building each new list. When the input list is empty, the final one is generated. Thus, we avoid any kind of counter to know when we are finished. For example, consider a call to `interleave` in our example:

$$
\begin{array}{rl}
& \text{interleave 1 [] [2; 3]} \\
\Longrightarrow & \text{([] @ [1; 2; 3]) :: interleave 1 ([] @ [2]) [3]} \\
\Longrightarrow & \text{[1; 2; 3] :: interleave 1 [2] [3]} \\
\Longrightarrow & \text{[1; 2; 3] :: (([2] @ 1 :: 3 :: []) :: interleave 1 ([2] @ [3]) [])} \\
\Longrightarrow & \text{[1; 2; 3] :: ([2; 1; 3] :: interleave 1 [2; 3] [])} \\
\Longrightarrow & \text{[1; 2; 3] :: ([2; 1; 3] :: [[2; 3] @ [1]])} \\
\Longrightarrow & \text{[[1; 2; 3]; [2; 1; 3]; [2; 3; 1]]} \\
\end{array}
$$

Now we can write the whole thing out:

Chapter 10. Finding Permutations

```
interleave : α → α list → α list → α list list
combine : α → α list list → α list
perms : α list → α list list

let rec interleave e seen l =
  match l with
    [] -> [seen @ [e]]
  | x::xs -> (seen @ e :: x :: xs) :: interleave e (seen @ [x]) xs

let combine x ps =
  List.concat (List.map (interleave x []) ps)

let rec perms p =
  match p with
    [] -> [[]]
  | h::t -> combine h (perms t)
```

Here are the 24 permutations of the list [1; 3; 5; 7]:

```
# perms [1; 3; 5; 7];;
- : int list list =
[[1; 3; 5; 7]; [3; 1; 5; 7]; [3; 5; 1; 7]; [3; 5; 7; 1]; [1; 5; 3; 7];
 [5; 1; 3; 7]; [5; 3; 1; 7]; [5; 3; 7; 1]; [1; 5; 7; 3]; [5; 1; 7; 3];
 [5; 7; 1; 3]; [5; 7; 3; 1]; [1; 3; 7; 5]; [3; 1; 7; 5]; [3; 7; 1; 5];
 [3; 7; 5; 1]; [1; 7; 3; 5]; [7; 1; 3; 5]; [7; 3; 1; 5]; [7; 3; 5; 1];
 [1; 7; 5; 3]; [7; 1; 5; 3]; [7; 5; 1; 3]; [7; 5; 3; 1]]
```

Note that our function does not work properly when there are duplicates in the list – it will treat each item as if it were different:

```
# perms [1; 1; 2];;
- : int list list =
[[1; 1; 2]; [1; 1; 2]; [1; 2; 1]; [1; 2; 1]; [2; 1; 1]; [2; 1; 1]]
```

In this implementation, we run into problems with the lack of tail recursion well before we run out of memory to store the permutations:

```
# List.length (perms [1; 2; 3; 4; 5; 6; 7; 8]);;
- : int = 40320
# List.length (perms [1; 2; 3; 4; 5; 6; 7; 8; 9]);;
- : int = 362880
# List.length (perms [1; 2; 3; 4; 5; 6; 7; 8; 9; 10]);;
Stack overflow during evaluation (looping recursion?).
```

To fix this up, we must rewrite `interleave` to be tail recursive by adding an accumulating argument:

```
interleave : α → α list → α list → α list list

let rec interleave acc e seen l =
  match l with
    [] -> (seen @ [e]) :: acc
  | x::xs ->
      interleave ((seen @ e :: x :: xs) :: acc) e (seen @ [x]) xs
```

Now, we can go as far as we have time and memory (though the permutations are in a different order – can you fix that?)

Another method of finding permutations, which gives a shorter solution, is to choose each element of the input list and use that as the first element, prepending it to each of the permutations of the remaining list. First, let us define a function to remove the (first) occurrence of a given element from a list:

```
without : α → α list → α list

let rec without x l =
  match l with
    [] -> []
  | h::t -> if h = x then t else h :: without x t
```

It need not be tail-recursive, since this list will always be small. Now, we can write the new `perms` function. The base case is the same. In the main case, we use `List.map` twice. The inner `map` prepends a given element to each of the permutations of the list without that element. The outer `map` uses that over each of the elements of the input, selecting each in turn as the first element. The results are then concatenated.

```
perms : α list → α list list

let rec perms l =
  match l with
    [] -> [[]]
  | l ->
      List.concat
        (List.map
          (fun x ->
            List.map (fun l -> x :: l) (perms (without x l)))
          l)
```

This function has the advantage of producing the items in proper lexicographic (dictionary) order:

[[1; 2; 3]; [1; 3; 2]; [2; 1; 3]; [2; 3; 1]; [3; 1; 2]; [3; 2; 1]]

Permutations one at a time

There is a well-known imperative algorithm for generating the lexicographically-next permutation given the current one. We can use this to build a function to generate all the permutations without the heavy recursion of our previous programs and, more interestingly, to build a lazy list of all the permutations, which requires minimal computation each time a new permutation is needed.

We begin with a sorted array, such as [|1; 2; 3|]. This is the first permutation. We generate new permutations until the array is in reverse-sorted order – [|3; 2; 1|] – this is the final permutation. In order to find the lexicographically-next permutation there are four steps:

1. Find the right-most item which is smaller than its next item. Call this the "first" item. This is the item which must be altered to find the permutation which is the smallest distance from the current one in the lexicographic order.

2. Find the smallest item to the right of the "first" item which is greater than it. Call this the "last" item. This is the item which will go in the position of the "first" item.

3. Swap these two characters.

4. Sort everything to the right of the original index of the "first" item into lexicographic order. This ensures we have selected the next permutation, not any later one.

Marking the first item with F and the last item with L, we have [|1; 2^F; 3^L|] $\longrightarrow$ [|1^F; 3; 2^L|] $\longrightarrow$ [|2; 1^F; 3^L|] $\longrightarrow$ [|2^F; 3^L; 1|] $\longrightarrow$ [|3; 1^F; 2^L|] $\longrightarrow$ [|3; 2; 1|]. The first function finds the index of the "first item" in an array:

```
first : α array → int

let first arr =
  let f = ref (Array.length arr - 1) in
    for x = 0 to Array.length arr - 2 do
      if arr.(x) < arr.(x + 1) then f := x
    done;
    !f
```

The corresponding last function is a little more awkward, needing to check two conditions and using a special initializer, rather than simply initializing with the last element as first does.

```
last : α array → int → int

let last arr f =
  let c = ref (-1) in
    for x = Array.length arr - 1 downto f + 1 do
      if arr.(x) > arr.(f) && (!c = (-1) || arr.(x) < arr.(!c))
        then c := x
    done;
    !c
```

Two simple utility functions, to swap given indices in an array, and sort a sub-array given its offset and length:

```
swap : α array → int → int → unit
sort_subarray : α array → int → int → unit

let swap arr a b =
  let t = arr.(a) in
    arr.(a) <- arr.(b);
    arr.(b) <- t

let sort_subarray arr o l =
  let sub = Array.sub arr o l in
    Array.sort compare sub;
    Array.blit sub 0 arr o l
```

Now we are ready to write next_permutation:

```
next_permutation : α array → α array

let next_permutation arr_in =
  let arr = Array.copy arr_in in
  let f = first arr in
  let c = last arr f in
    swap arr f c;
    sort_subarray arr (f + 1) (Array.length arr - 1 - f);
    arr
```

We define a predicate for non-increasing-ness:

```
non_increasing : α array → bool

let non_increasing arr =
  Array.length arr <= 1 ||
  let r = ref true in
    for x = 0 to Array.length arr - 2 do
      if arr.(x + 1) > arr.(x) then r := false
    done;
    !r
```

And, finally, we are finished:

Chapter 10. Finding Permutations

```
all_permutations : α array → α array array

let all_permutations arr =
  let copy = Array.copy arr in
    Array.sort compare copy;
    let perm = ref copy in
    let perms = ref [copy] in
      while not (non_increasing !perm) do
        perm := next_permutation !perm;
        perms := !perm :: !perms;
      done;
      Array.of_list (List.rev !perms)
```

Note that this imperative algorithm works correctly with repetitions of elements – it will include the permutation only once. We can now generate a repeating lazy list of all the permutations of a given list, using our standard lazy list type from Chapter 2:

```
perms : α array → α array lazylist

let rec perms x =
  Cons (x, fun () ->
    if non_increasing x then
      let c = Array.copy x in
        Array.sort compare c;
        perms c
    else
      perms (next_permutation x))
```

This very imperative algorithm has now been dressed in functional clothes.

Questions

1. Write a function to generate all the unordered combinations of items from a list. For example, for the list [1; 2; 3], the result, whose order is not important, might be [[]; [1]; [2]; [3]; [1; 2]; [1, 3]; [2; 3]; [1; 2; 3]].

2. Generate all the "permicombinations" – that is all the permutations of all the combinations of a list. For the list [1; 2; 3] this might be [[]; [1]; [2]; [3]; [1; 2]; [2; 1]; [1; 3]; [3; 1]; [2; 3]; [3; 2]; [1; 2; 3]].

3. Write a function to give the list of all possible lists of length n containing just `true` and `false`.

4. The sorting phase of the imperative algorithm can be replaced with a simple list reversal, since the items are already in reverse lexicographic order each after the swap. Implement this.

5. The imperative algorithm could be defined in terms of lists, in a functional fashion. Demonstrate this.

Chapter 11

Making Sets

In this chapter, we will look at various naive and sophisticated data structures for storing sets. We will look at their theoretical performance characteristics and time them against one another on various sorts of data to learn about their performance in practice. Along the way, we will learn about some of OCaml's more advanced modular abstraction mechanisms. For each set representation, we will give the following five functions:

- `set_of_list` which builds a set from a list (which may contain duplicates). The empty set is built with `set_of_list []`;

- `list_of_set` which returns, in no particular order, a list of the elements in the set;

- `insert` which inserts a given element into the set, if it is not already present;

- `size` which returns the number of elements in the set; and

- `member` which tests if an element is present in the set.

Simple lists

Figure 11.1 exhibits these five functions by representing sets using the built-in **list** type. They are largely trivial, save for `set_of_list` which works by repeated insertion into the existing set.

These functions are not terribly efficient. The `member`, `size`, and `insert` functions take time proportional to the size of the set. The `set_of_list` function is worse: it takes time proportional to the square of the size of the set, since it uses `insert` for each element on a growing list. The only bright spot is `list_of_set` which (of course) runs in constant time.

We have not hidden the type of the sets – they may be manipulated by the caller as plain lists – and so the abstraction is not safe or complete. Here is an interface as a `.mli` file, abstracting the real type of the set to just $\alpha\,t$.

```
member : α → α list → bool
insert : α → α list → α list
set_of_list : α list → α list
list_of_set : α → α
size : α list → int

let member = List.mem

let insert x l =
  if member x l then l else x :: l

let rec set_of_list l =
  match l with [] -> [] | h::t -> insert h (set_of_list t)

let list_of_set x = x

let size = List.length
```

Figure 11.1

```
type 'a t

val set_of_list : 'a list -> 'a t

val list_of_set : 'a t -> 'a list

val insert : 'a -> 'a t -> 'a t

val size : 'a t -> int

val member : 'a -> 'a t -> bool
```

Here is the corresponding .ml file with the implementation:

```
type 'a t = 'a list

let member = List.mem

let insert x l =
  if member x l then l else x :: l

let rec set_of_list l =
  match l with [] -> [] | h::t -> insert h (set_of_list t)

let list_of_set x = x

let size = List.length
```

Chapter 11. Making Sets

```ocaml
module SetList :
  sig
    type 'a t
    val set_of_list : 'a list -> 'a t
    val list_of_set : 'a t -> 'a list
    val insert : 'a -> 'a t -> 'a t
    val size : 'a t -> int
    val member : 'a -> 'a t -> bool
  end
=
  struct
    type 'a t = 'a list

    let member = List.mem

    let insert x l =
      if member x l then l else x :: l

    let rec set_of_list l =
      match l with [] -> [] | h::t -> insert h (set_of_list t)

    let list_of_set x = x

    let size = List.length
  end
```

Figure 11.2

Recall that, by hiding the implementation behind an interface, we can swap implementations at will, making them more efficient, or fixing bugs.

Since we wish to build several of these set implementations, and benchmark them, it is a good time to look at OCaml's syntax for putting several modules in a single source file. Figure 11.2 exhibits a piece of OCaml which corresponds to our .ml and .mli file all in one place:

The general syntactic form is:

module *module name* :
  sig
    contents of .mli file
  end
=
  struct
    contents of .ml file
  end

When this code is pasted into the top level, or loaded in some other way, a new module SetList is available, with functions like SetList.size available through the given interface.

Since all our different implementations of sets will share the same interface as SetList, we will split this module definition up using the **module type** syntax to define the signature, and the **include** keyword to use that signature for our module:

```
module type SetType =
  sig
    type 'a t
    val set_of_list : 'a list -> 'a t
    val list_of_set : 'a t -> 'a list
    val insert : 'a -> 'a t -> 'a t
    val size : 'a t -> int
    val member : 'a -> 'a t -> bool
  end

module SetList : sig include SetType end =
  struct
    type 'a t = 'a list

    let list_of_set x = x

    let insert x l = x :: l

    let rec set_of_list l =
      match l with [] -> [] | h::t -> insert h (set_of_list t)

    let size = List.length

    let member = List.mem
  end
```

Thus, we have avoided duplication of the interface. Each new set representation will just need an implementation.

Performance

Each use of the set data type is different – sometimes there is an initial phase of insertions, followed by millions of membership tests with no insertions. Sometimes insertions and membership tests are equally likely. Some functions may not be required at all. We shall consider two benchmarks for insertion:

- the insertion of the integers 1...50000 in a randomized order; and
- the insertion, in order, of the 50000 integers 1...50000.

Then, we will, for each of these "ordered" and "unordered" cases:

- perform 50000 membership tests in the range of numbers 1...100000, so that half are present and half not;
- calculate the number of elements in the set;
- calculate the size of the set.

Here are the results:

Chapter 11. Making Sets

(sets represented with lists)	Unordered	Ordered
Insertion	20.5s	17.5s
Membership	34.7s	17.8s
Elements	0s	0s
Size	0s	0s

The big difference is in the time for the membership tests, due to the balance or lack of balance in the tree, as expected. When we introduce more ways of storing sets, we will do the same tests, and compare the results.

Binary Search Trees

A binary search tree is a binary tree with the property that all elements in the left sub-tree of each node are smaller than it, and all elements in the right sub-tree are larger. If the tree is reasonably well balanced, we can reach any element in time proportional to the logarithm of the number of elements in the set.

Just like the representation of sets, there are multiple representations of sets, depending upon the order of insertion of the elements. Here are the trees corresponding to the insertion orders 123, 132, 213, 231, 312, 321:

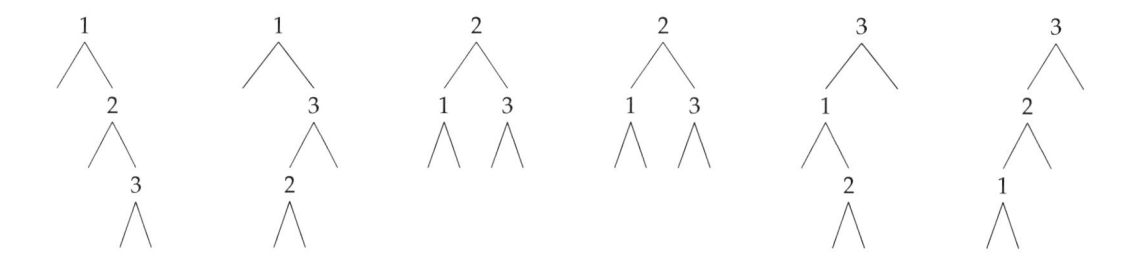

We can see that when the items in the set are added in numerical or reverse-numerical order, this data structure is equivalent to, and has no better performance, than a simple list. The data type is the usual one for binary trees:

type 'a t = Lf | Br **of** 'a t * 'a * 'a t

The SetTree module is shown in Figure 11.3.

When the tree is balanced `insert` and `member` run in logarithmic time. The `size` function runs in linear time, since it must visit every node irrespective of the balance. The same is true of `list_of_set`. When unbalanced, `insert` and `member` take linear time. We can extend our table now:

```ocaml
module SetTree : sig include SetType end =
  struct
    type 'a t = Lf | Br of 'a t * 'a * 'a t

    let rec list_of_set s =
      match s with
        Lf -> []
      | Br (l, x, r) -> list_of_set l @ [x] @ list_of_set r

    let rec insert x s =
      match s with
        Lf -> Br (Lf, x, Lf)
    | Br (l, y, r) ->
         if x = y then Br (l, y, r)
         else if x < y then Br (insert x l, y, r)
         else Br (l, y, insert x r)

    let rec set_of_list l =
      match l with
        [] -> Lf
      | h::t -> insert h (set_of_list t)

    let rec size s =
      match s with
        Lf -> 0
      | Br (l, _, r) -> 1 + size l + size r

    let rec member x s =
      match s with
        Lf -> false
      | Br (_, y, _) when x = y -> true
      | Br (l, y, r) -> if x < y then member x l else member x r
  end
```

Figure 11.3

Chapter 11. Making Sets

	Unordered	Ordered		Unordered	Ordered
(Sets represented with lists)			*(Sets represented with trees)*		
Insertion	20.4s	17.5s	Insertion	0.09s	116.6s
Membership	34.8s	17.8s	Membership	0.02s	33.4s
Elements	0s	0s	Elements	0.02s	98.0s
Size	0s	0s	Size	0s	0s

Notice that, in the unordered case, performance is dramatically increased for insertion and membership, by about two hundred times. However, if the elements are inserted in order, the unbalanced tree actually takes longer to build than its equivalent list. Finding all the elements as a list also takes a huge amount of time in the ordered insertion case.

Balanced trees

We have seen that binary search trees are only useful if they are reasonably close to balanced. In recent decades, several data structures have been developed which try to keep a binary tree "reasonably balanced", such that operations remain efficient. "Red-Black trees" are one such commonly used and interesting data structure. Red-Black trees were invented by Rudolf Bayer, and the functional formulation presented here is due to Chris Okasaki in his landmark book *"Purely Functional Data Structures"* (Cambridge University Press, 1998).

A Red-Black tree is an ordinary binary tree with one addition: each node is either Red or Black. Leaf nodes are considered Black. The balance is ensured by every operation which alters the tree (in our case, just `insert`) so that the following remains true:

- the children of each Red node are Black; and
- each path from root to leaf contains an equal number of Black nodes.

These two rules, together, ensure that the tree is reasonably balanced – the longest path from root to leaf (Black, Red, Black, Red ... Black) is no more than twice as long as the shortest path (Black, Black, Black ... Black). Thus, the maximum depth of a Red-Black tree is proportional to the logarithm of the number of elements in the set. Here is an example valid Red-Black tree, with 3 black nodes in each path:

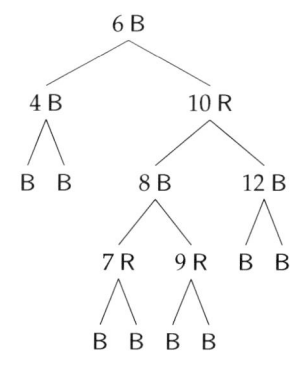

```
              6 B
            /     \
         4 B      10 R
         / \      /    \
       B   B   8 B    12 B
               / \     / \
             7 R  9 R B   B
             / \  / \
            B  B B  B
```

Here are the types for representing a Red-Black tree – we have just added a new colour field to each branch of the tree:

```
type colour = R | B

type 'a t = Lf | Br of colour * 'a t * 'a * 'a t
```

The `list_of_set`, `size`, and `member` functions are simple to alter: they just ignore the colour field. The `insert` function, however, must be modified to preserve the Red-Black properties.

As with ordinary binary search trees, the new node added by `insert` will be in place of a leaf node. We colour it Red, to make sure that the invariant that no path can have a differing number of black nodes in it is not broken. However, this may break the other invariant (that no Red node has a Red parent). It turns out that, by considering the parent and grandparent of the newly-inserted node, performing a simple operation, and possibly continuing this process upward, we can restore this invariant, and efficiently. The following diagrams, à la Okasaki, illustrate the process:

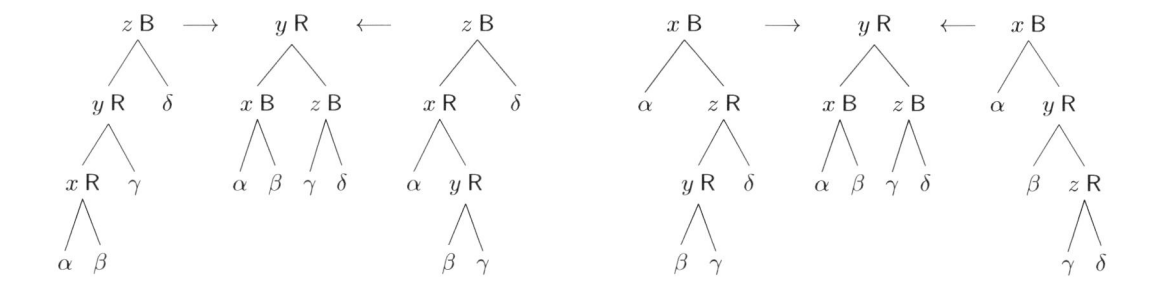

In each case, the nodes x, y, z and the sub-trees $\alpha, \beta, \gamma, \delta$ remain in the same order, so the binary tree invariant is preserved. Pattern matching is particularly elegant here, since all but one of our cases have the same result:

```
balance : colour × α t × α × α t → α t

let balance t =
  match t with
    (B, Br (R, Br (R, a, x, b), y, c), z, d)
  | (B, Br (R, a, x, Br (R, b, y, c)), z, d)
  | (B, a, x, Br (R, Br (R, b, y, c), z, d))
  | (B, a, x, Br (R, b, y, Br (R, c, z, d))) ->
      Br (R, Br (B, a, x, b), y, Br (B, c, z, d))
  | (a, b, c, d) -> Br (a, b, c, d)
```

Now, we can write the insertion function itself:

Chapter 11. Making Sets

```
insert_inner : α → α t → α t
insert : α → α t → α t

let rec insert_inner x s =
  match s with
    Lf -> Br (R, Lf, x, Lf)
  | Br (c, l, y, r) ->
      if x < y
        then balance (c, insert_inner x l, y, r)
        else if x > y then balance (c, l, y, insert_inner x r)
        else Br (c, l, y, r)

let insert x s =
  match insert_inner x s with
    Br (_, l, y, r) -> Br (B, l, y, r)
  | Lf -> assert false
```

Note that we wrap it in a function to set the root of the tree to Black – balancing will not do this, since the root has no parent or grandparent to compare with, and so we may otherwise end up with a red root with a red child. The full module is shown in Figure 11.4.

Since we have guaranteed that the tree will be reasonably balanced, there is no need for tail recursive functions, even for huge sets. The effect of balanced trees on performance is clear, and there appears to be little or no slow-down from the more complex Red-Black data structure:

	Unordered	Ordered		Unordered	Ordered
(Sets represented with lists)			*(Sets represented with trees)*		
Insertion	20.4s	17.5s	Insertion	0.09s	116.6s
Membership	34.8s	17.8s	Membership	0.02s	33.4s
Elements	0s	0s	Elements	0.02s	98.0s
Size	0s	0s	Size	0s	0s

	Unordered	Ordered
(Sets represented with Red-Black trees)		
Insertion	0.11s	0.05s
Membership	0.02s	0.02s
Elements	0.03s	0.01s
Size	0s	0s

```ocaml
module SetRedBlack : sig include SetType end =
  struct
    type colour = R | B

    type 'a t = Lf | Br of colour * 'a t * 'a * 'a t

    let rec list_of_set s =
      match s with
        Lf -> []
      | Br (_, l, x, r) -> x :: list_of_set l @ list_of_set r

    let balance t =
      match t with
        (B, Br (R, Br (R, a, x, b), y, c), z, d)
      | (B, Br (R, a, x, Br (R, b, y, c)), z, d)
      | (B, a, x, Br (R, Br (R, b, y, c), z, d))
      | (B, a, x, Br (R, b, y, Br (R, c, z, d))) ->
          Br (R, Br (B, a, x, b), y, Br (B, c, z, d))
      | (a, b, c, d) -> Br (a, b, c, d)

    let rec insert_inner x s =
      match s with
        Lf -> Br (R, Lf, x, Lf)
      | Br (c, l, y, r) ->
          if x < y
            then balance (c, insert_inner x l, y, r)
            else if x > y then balance (c, l, y, insert_inner x r)
            else Br (c, l, y, r)

    let insert x s =
      match insert_inner x s with
        Br (_, l, y, r) -> Br (B, l, y, r)
      | Lf -> assert false

    let rec set_of_list l =
      match l with
        [] -> Lf
      | h::t -> insert h (set_of_list t)

    let rec size s =
      match s with
        Lf -> 0
      | Br (_, l, _, r) -> 1 + size l + size r

    let rec member x s =
      match s with
        Lf -> false
      | Br (_, l, y, r) ->
          x = y || if x > y then member x r else member x l
  end
```

Figure 11.4

Hash Tables

A *hash table* is a data structure designed to provide very fast insertion of and access to data in sets and maps. It holds a set of *buckets* $0...n$. When we insert a value into the set, it is processed via a *hash function* which allocates it to a bucket, in such a manner that there should be a roughly uniform distribution of values among the buckets. When we need to test membership for an item, the same hash function is applied, and we need only search in one bucket. If the hash function works well and the number of buckets is appropriate, lookup is in constant time regardless of how many items are in the set.

For example, if the hash function is $x \longrightarrow x$ mod 23 and the data to be inserted is 34, 2, 67, 3, 4, 84, 1467, 7432, 48, 1 then the buckets would be 11, 2, 21, 3, 4, 15, 18, 3, 1, 1. The membership test for 67 now consists of applying the hash function, and then searching in bucket 21 to see if 67 is there.

The OCaml Standard Library provides a hash table implementation in the module **Hashtbl**. To build a hash table for a set, we use a hash table which maps from α to **unit**, of type (α, **unit**) **Hashtbl.t**. It is simple to build an implementation matching our signature, using the functions Hashtbl.mem, Hashtbl.add, Hashtbl.create, and Hashtbl.iter, as shown in Figure 11.5.

The disadvantage is that hash tables are mutable data structures, and so operations like insert mutate the structure. The result of insert, then, alters the set rather than creating a new set. This means that whilst the SetType interface is technically satisfied, our intended abstraction is actually broken. Such is mutability. The performance on our benchmarks, however, is clear:

	Unordered	Ordered		Unordered	Ordered
(Sets represented with lists)			*(Sets represented with trees)*		
Insertion	20.4s	17.5s	Insertion	0.09s	116.6s
Membership	34.8s	17.8s	Membership	0.02s	33.4s
Elements	0s	0s	Elements	0.02s	98.0s
Size	0s	0s	Size	0s	0s

	Unordered	Ordered		Unordered	Ordered
(Sets represented with Red-Black trees)			*(Sets represented with hash tables)*		
Insertion	0.11s	0.06s	Insertion	0.014s	0.007s
Membership	0.01s	0.02s	Membership	0.012	0.005s
Elements	0.03s	0.01s	Elements	0.004s	0.0022s
Size	0s	0s	Size	0s	0s

The benchmarking programs may be found in the online resources.

```ocaml
module SetHashtbl : sig include SetType end =
  struct
    type 'a t = ('a, unit) Hashtbl.t

    let list_of_set s =
      Hashtbl.fold (fun x () l -> x ::  l) s []

    let set_of_list l =
      let s = Hashtbl.create (List.length l) in
        List.iter (fun x -> Hashtbl.add s x ()) l;
        s

    let member x s = Hashtbl.mem s x

    let insert x s =
      if not (member x s) then Hashtbl.add s x ();
      s

    let size = Hashtbl.length
  end
```

Figure 11.5

Questions

1. Compare our set representations with regard to the amount of memory required to create and store them. You can use the functions from the **Gc** module in OCaml's Standard Library to find out how many words of memory have been allocated before and after allocating a large set in each set representation.

2. Write functions (naive if necessary) to perform the "union" operation on sets in each representation. The union of two sets is the set of elements present in one or the other or both of them. After the operation, both inputs should still be available as sets.

3. OCaml has a built-in **Set** module. It uses advanced module syntax not discussed here, but you can build a module for manipulating sets of integers like this:

   `module S = Set.Make (struct type t = int let compare = compare end)`

   This new module S provides, amongst others, a type t for sets, and `add`, `elements`, `mem`, `empty`, and `cardinal` functions, whose definitions you can find in the OCaml manual. Use these functions to build a set module with a similar interface to ours. Comment on its speed for our examples.

4. We can save memory in the definition of Red-Black trees by having two different `Br` nodes, one for Red and one for Black, instead of storing the colour. Implement this. How much memory is saved? How much extra complexity is there in the source code?

Chapter 12

Playing Games

The childhood game of Noughts and Crosses is a combinatorial problem of a large but manageable size. Let us review the rules, and then see if we can build the *game tree* (that is, a structure describing all possible games), and draw some statistics from it.

A 3-by-3 grid is constructed. Two players (O and X) take turns, beginning with O, to place their piece in an empty space. The game is won if or when a player forms three pieces in a row, column, or diagonally. The game is drawn if the board is full and no such pattern has been formed. For example, in this board, player O has won, building a diagonal:

	X	O
X	O	X
O	X	O

Let us consider the shape of the game tree. Clearly, at the top level, it will branch nine ways, since O can be placed in any square. Then eight ways, seven ways and so on. Once we reach the fifth level, some of the games have been won (since three pieces from player O may form a line), and so the number of branches may be reduced. The tree must end after nine levels, since the board must at least be full, even if no-one has won. A fragment of the game tree is shown in Figure 12.1. Let us begin to construct the program. We will need a type to represent X, O and the empty square:

```
type turn = O | X | E
```

It would be natural to use a nine-tuple, since the board is of a fixed size. Then, though, we lose the ability to use the standard list-processing functions such as `List.map` over the boards. So, at the cost of a little inelegance, we will use a list of length nine instead – in other words a `turn list`.

We need to terminate the tree when X has won, O has won, or the board is full. Thus we will need to check all the rows, columns, and diagonals. We do not want to replicate the logic several times or build a huge pattern match, so it is easiest to write a function which takes a list of nine booleans and just checks for lines of `true`. We can then use `List.map` on the board itself to build these intermediate lists of booleans.

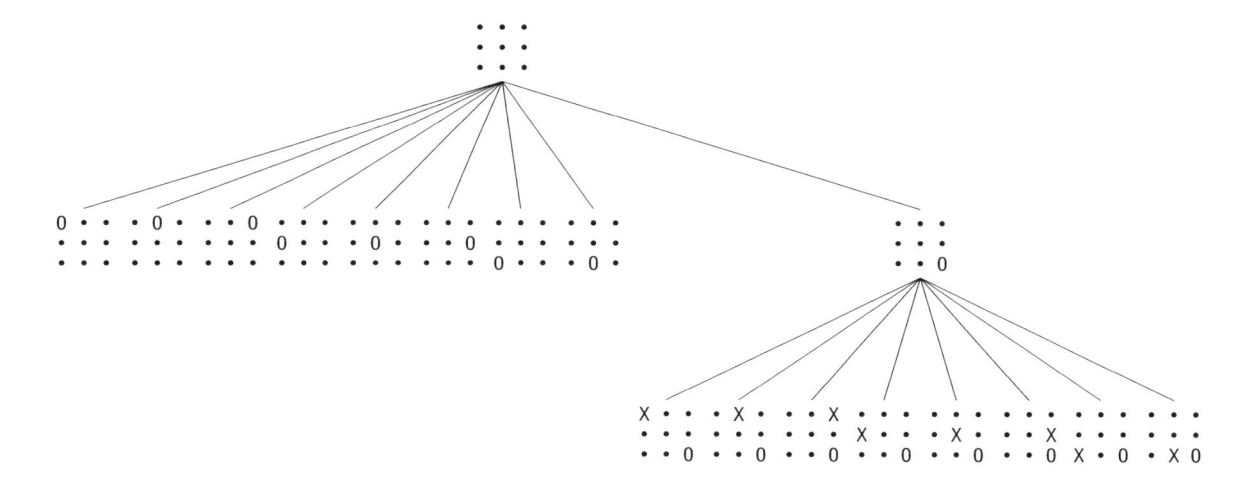

[Figure 12.1 diagram showing a game tree of tic-tac-toe board positions]

Figure 12.1

```
won : bool list → bool

let won [a; b; c; d; e; f; g; h; i] =
  a && b && c || d && e && f || g && h && i || a && d && g ||
  b && e && h || c && f && i || a && e && i || c && e && g
```

We can number the positions in our board:

1	2	3
4	5	6
7	8	9

Now, we can use functions from the **List** module to write a function to return the numbers of the positions which are currently empty:

```
empty : turn → int list

let empty b =
  List.map snd
    (List.filter (fun (t, _) -> t = E)
      (List.combine b [1; 2; 3; 4; 5; 6; 7; 8; 9]))
```

This works by building the list of tuples [(X, 1); (E, 2); (E, 3) ... (O, 9)], filtering out any which are not empty, and extracting the list of empty positions [2, 3 ...]. It is also simple to write a function which, given a board like [E; E; E; E; X; E; O; E; E], a turn like O and a number such as 8, will fill in the correct slot in the board to produce [E; E; E; E; X; E; O; X; E]. The take and drop functions from our Util module (described on page xiii) are ideal:

Chapter 12. Playing Games

```
replace : turn → turn list → int → turn list

let replace turn board p =
  Util.take board (p - 1) @ [turn] @ Util.drop board p
```

One more simple function is required before we can write the main tree-building function, and that is to change whose turn it is:

```
flip_turn : turn → turn

let flip_turn t =
  match t with O -> X | X -> O
```

What should the type of the game tree be? Each node needs a list of turn elements representing the board, and a list of zero or more trees representing the game resulting from each possible move. Since the list can have zero elements, we need no separate leaf constructor:

```
type tree = Move of turn list * tree list
```

Now we may construct the main function. Our job is to build, given a turn (X or O) and the current board, the tree starting at that board. If the board has been won by either player, the list of next nodes is empty, and the recursion stops. If not, we calculate the empty positions, build a new board with each empty position filled in with the current turn, and then map next_moves over each of those.

```
next_moves : turn → turn list → tree

let rec next_moves turn board =
  let next =
    if
      won (List.map (( = ) O) board) ||
      won (List.map (( = ) X) board)
    then
      []
    else
      List.map
        (next_moves (flip_turn turn))
        (List.map (replace turn board) (empty board))
  in
    Move (board, next)
```

Note that the recursion stops when a board is full (drawn) because empty returns the empty list in this case. Now we can build the game tree itself, which might take a second or so:

```
game_tree : tree

let game_tree =
  next_moves O [E; E; E; E; E; E; E; E; E]
```

This results in the tree shown below.

```
val game_tree : tree =
  Move ([E; E; E; E; E; E; E; E; E],
    [Move ([O; E; E; E; E; E; E; E; E],
      [Move ([O; X; E; E; E; E; E; E; E],
        [Move ([O; X; O; E; E; E; E; E; E],
          [Move ([O; X; O; X; E; E; E; E; E],
            [Move ([O; X; O; X; O; E; E; E; E],
              [Move ([O; X; O; X; O; X; E; E; E],
                [Move ([O; X; O; X; O; X; O; E; E], []);
                Move ([O; X; O; X; O; X; E; O; E],
                  [Move ([O; X; O; X; O; X; X; O;
                    [Move ([O; X; O; X; O; X; X; O; O], [])]);
                  Move ([O; X; O; X; O; X; E; O; X],
                    [Move ([O; X; O; X; O; X; O; O; X], [])])]);
                Move ([O; X; O; X; O; X; E; E; O], [])]);
              Move ([O; X; O; X; O; E; X; E; E],
                [Move ([O; X; O; X; O; O; X; E; E],
                  [Move ([O; X; O; X; O; O; X; X; E],
                    [Move ([O; X; O; X; O; O; X; X; O], [])]);
                  Move ([O; X; O; X; O; O; X; E; X],
                    [Move ([O; X; O; X; O; O; X; O; X], [])])]);
                Move ([O; X; O; X; O; E; X; O; E],
                  [Move ([O; X; O; X; O; X; X; O; E],
                    [Move ([O; X; O; X; O; X; X; O; O], [])]);
                  Move ([O; X; O; X; O; E; X; O; X],
                    [Move ([O; X; O; X; O; O; X; O; X], [])])]);
                ...]);
              ...]);
            ...]);
          ...]);
        ...]);
      ...]);
    ...])
```

You can see the first ending position in this game tree is [O; X; O; X; O; X; O; E; E]. You can also see several drawn games. We can now use this game tree to calculate how many games are won by a given player:

```
num_wins : term → tree → int

let rec num_wins turn (Move (b, bs)) =
  (if won (List.map (( = ) turn) b) then 1 else 0) +
  List.fold_left ( + ) 0 (List.map (num_wins turn) bs)
```

This tells us, reasonably quickly, that O wins 131184 games. The questions at the end of this chapter ask you to work out more of these numbers. Here is the full code in one place:

Chapter 12. Playing Games

```
type turn = O | X | E

let won [a; b; c; d; e; f; g; h; i] =
  a && b && c || d && e && f || g && h && i || a && d && g ||
  b && e && h || c && f && i || a && e && i || c && e && g

let replace turn board p =
  Util.take board (p - 1) @ [turn] @ Util.drop board p

let flip_turn t =
  match t with O -> X | X -> O

let empty b =
  List.map snd
    (List.filter (fun (t, _) -> t = E)
      (List.combine b [1; 2; 3; 4; 5; 6; 7; 8; 9]))

type tree = Move of turn list * tree list

let rec next_moves turn board =
  let next =
    if
      won (List.map (( = ) O) board) ||
      won (List.map (( = ) X) board)
    then
      []
    else
      List.map
        (next_moves (flip_turn turn))
        (List.map (replace turn board) (empty board))
  in
    Move (board, next)

let game_tree =
  next_moves O [E; E; E; E; E; E; E; E; E]
```

In the questions, you will extract the rest of the statistics from the tree, and build some alternative representations.

Questions

1. In how many cases does X win? How many possible different games are there? How many end in a draw?

2. Build a lazy version of our game tree, where nodes are only created when explored. Now write a function to work out how many times O and X win or the game is drawn if O goes first and picks the centre slot. What about if O picks a corner? The middle of a side?

3. Another way to check if someone has won is to rearrange the board numbers into a so-called *magic square*, where each row, column or diagonal sums to 15:

8	1	6
3	5	7
4	9	2

    Now, a player has won if they have any three positions summing to 15. Re-implement our game tree program using this alternative representation.

Generating PDF Documents

an extended example

Chapter 13

Representing Documents

In this chapter we will define a data type for representing a PDF document. PDF is a structured format for describing a wide variety of graphical and textual data. The PDF file format itself is large and complex, but we will introduce only the parts required for our examples. It is relatively easy to write PDF files but rather harder to read them, so we will concentrate on creating PDF data structures in memory, and then writing them to valid files. Here is an example PDF, as it might be displayed in a PDF viewer:

Hello, World!

Here is the corresponding code, which you would see if you opened the PDF file in a plain text editor:

```
%PDF-1.1
1 0 obj
<</Type /Page
  /Parent 3 0 R
  /Resources
```

```
    <</Font
       <</F0
          <</Type /Font /Subtype /Type1 /BaseFont /Times-Italic>>>>>>
       /MediaBox [0 0 595.275590551 841.88976378]
       /Rotate 0 /Contents [4 0 R] >>
endobj
2 0 obj
<</Type /Catalog /Pages 3 0 R>>
endobj
3 0 obj
<</Type /Pages /Kids [1 0 R] /Count 1>>
endobj
4 0 obj
<</Length 53>>
stream
1 0 0 1 50 770 cm BT /F0 36 Tf (Hello, World!) Tj ET
endstream
endobj
xref
0 5
0000000000 65535 f
0000000015 00000 n
0000000200 00000 n
0000000245 00000 n
0000000296 00000 n
trailer
<</Size 5 /Root 2 0 R>>
startxref
397
%%EOF
```

Rather complicated, as we can see. Our first job is to define a pleasant OCaml data type for PDF documents, which can then be flattened to the format above when written to a file.

The main body of a PDF file is a set of numbered objects – there are four in the example above, from `1 0 obj` to `4 0 obj`. Each one contains some structured data, such as the *dictionary* `<</Type /Pages /Kids [1 0 R] /Count 1>>` which associates the keys `/Type`, `/Kids`, and `/Count` to the name `/Pages`, the array `[1 0 R]`, and the integer `1` respectively. Before and after the main body is some ancillary data, most of which we do not need to hold in our data structure – it is generated upon writing. Here are all the kinds of data we will be using:

- Booleans, like `true` and `false`
- Integers, such as $4, 256, -1$
- Floating-point numbers such as 1.585
- Strings, like `(a string)` which are sequences of characters within parentheses
- Names, like `/Name`
- Ordered arrays of objects such as `[1 2 4]`
- Dictionaries, which are unordered collections of key-value pairs, where the keys are names. For example, `<</One 1 /Two 2 /Three 3>>`.

Chapter 13. Representing Documents

- Streams, like object 4 in the example above, which are arbitrary sequences of bytes.
- Indirect references, like `4 0 R` which point to another object by its number (here, object 4).

Here is an OCaml data type to hold such data:

```
type pdfobject =
  Boolean of bool
| Integer of int
| Float of float
| String of string
| Name of string
| Array of pdfobject list
| Dictionary of (string * pdfobject) list
| Stream of pdfobject * string
| Indirect of int
```

Note that it is recursive, mirroring the structure of the data. For example, object 3 in the example above, that is <</Type /Pages /Kids [1 0 R] /Count 1>>, will be represented as:

```
Dictionary
  [("/Type", Name "/Pages"); ("/Kids", Array [Indirect 1]); ("/Count", Integer 1)]
```

Now, we need a type to represent the whole document, which contains a list of these objects, the PDF version number (1.1 in the example above), and the *trailer dictionary* (<</Size 5 /Root 2 0 R>> above). Everything else is generated upon writing. It is traditional to name the main type of a module t:

```
type t =
  {version : int * int;
   objects : (int * pdfobject) list;
   trailer : pdfobject}
```

We put these two types into `pdf.ml` and `pdf.mli`. Here is how we might build an instance of this data type representing our example PDF:

```
let objects =
  [(1,
    Pdf.Dictionary
      [("/Type", Pdf.Name "/Page");
       ("/Parent", Pdf.Indirect 3);
       ("/Resources",
          Pdf.Dictionary
            [("/Font",
              Pdf.Dictionary
                [("/F0",
                  Pdf.Dictionary
                    [("/Type", Pdf.Name "/Font");
                     ("/Subtype", Pdf.Name "/Type1");
                     ("/BaseFont", Pdf.Name "/Times-Italic")])])]);
       ("/MediaBox",
          Pdf.Array
            [Pdf.Float 0.; Pdf.Float 0.;
```

```
                  Pdf.Float 595.275590551; Pdf.Float 841.88976378]);
         ("/Rotate", Pdf.Integer 0);
         ("/Contents", Pdf.Array [Pdf.Indirect 4])]);
    (2,
      Pdf.Dictionary
        [("/Type", Pdf.Name "/Catalog");
         ("/Pages", Pdf.Indirect 3)]);
    (3,
      Pdf.Dictionary
        [("/Type", Pdf.Name "/Pages");
         ("/Kids", Pdf.Array [Pdf.Indirect 1]);
         ("/Count", Pdf.Integer 1)]);
    (4,
      Pdf.Stream
        (Pdf.Dictionary [("/Length", Pdf.Integer 53)],
         "1 0 0 1 50 770 cm BT /F0 36 Tf (Hello, World!) Tj ET"))]

let hello =
  {Pdf.version = (1, 1);
   Pdf.objects = objects;
   Pdf.trailer =
   Pdf.Dictionary
     [("/Size", Pdf.Integer 5);
      ("/Root", Pdf.Indirect 2)]}
```

The advantage of using this data structure as opposed to generating the PDF file directly is that it may be programmatically manipulated with ease, using pattern matching and other standard OCaml techniques. Note that the content of the page itself `"1 0 0 1 50 770 cm BT /F0 36 Tf (Hello, World!) Tj ET"` remains a plain string. We shall look at this separate language soon.

In the next three chapters, we will learn how to write this representation to a file, and add our own text and graphics to the page.

Chapter 13. Representing Documents

Questions

1. Draw the graph of the relationships, via indirect references such as 3 0 R, of the objects 1, 2, 3, 4 and the trailer dictionary.

2. Represent the following PDF objects using our data type:

   /Name

   (Quartz Crystal)

   <</Type /ObjStm /N 100 /First 807 /Length 1836 /Filter /FlateDecode>>

   [1 2 1.5 (black)]

   [1 2 0 R]

3. PDF files can contain arbitrary objects, which will be ignored by a PDF reader if they are not understood. Design a way of representing items of the following type using one or more PDF objects:

   type tree = Lf | Br **of** tree * int * tree

4. Write a function of type pdfobject → pdfobject which, given an object, replaces the value of any dictionary entry with key /Rotate to 90.

Chapter 14

Writing Documents

We have built a representation for PDF documents to be held in memory, and defined an example document. Now, we must build functions to write this to file. Recall our example file from the last chapter:

```
%PDF-1.1
1 0 obj
<</Type /Page
  /Parent 3 0 R
  /Resources
    <</Font
      <</F0
        <</Type /Font /Subtype /Type1 /BaseFont /Times-Italic>>>>>>
      /MediaBox [0 0 595.275590551 841.88976378]
      /Rotate 0 /Contents [4 0 R] >>
endobj
2 0 obj
<</Type /Catalog /Pages 3 0 R>>
endobj
3 0 obj
<</Type /Pages /Kids [1 0 R] /Count 1>>
endobj
4 0 obj
<</Length 53>>
stream
1 0 0 1 50 770 cm BT /F0 36 Tf (Hello, World!) Tj ET
endstream
endobj
xref
0 5
0000000000 65535 f
0000000015 00000 n
0000000200 00000 n
0000000245 00000 n
0000000296 00000 n
trailer
<</Size 5 /Root 2 0 R>>
```

```
startxref
397
%%EOF
```

It consists, we remember, of a *header*, then some *objects* (here, four), and a *trailer*. We will need four functions:

1. The function `string_of_pdfobject` to make a string from a Pdf.pdfobject, for example making the string "<</Type /Pages /Kids [1 0 R] /Count 1>>" from the pdfobject `Dictionary [("/Type", Name "/Pages"); ("/Kids", Array [Indirect 1]); ("/Count", Integer 1)]`;

2. The function `write_header` to write the header (i.e. everything before the objects);

3. The function `write_trailer` to write the trailer (i.e. everything after the objects); and

4. The main function `pdf_to_file` which uses these three functions to write a Pdf.t to a file under the given file name.

The function `string_of_pdfobject` is best expressed as a set of mutually-recursive functions introduced with the **let rec** ... **and** ... construct. To give it as a single function is possible, but would be rather large, and so harder to read and edit. Let us present it piece-by-piece and then all at once.

First, the main part. Given an object we wish to produce its string, assuming that `string_of_array`, `string_of_dictionary`, and `string_of_stream` exist:

---

string_of_pdfobject : Pdf.pdfobject → **string**

```
let rec string_of_pdfobject obj =
  match obj with
    Pdf.Boolean b -> string_of_bool b
  | Pdf.Integer i -> string_of_int i
  | Pdf.Float f -> string_of_float f
  | Pdf.String s -> "(" ^ s ^ ")"
  | Pdf.Name n -> n
  | Pdf.Array a -> string_of_array a
  | Pdf.Dictionary d -> string_of_dictionary d
  | Pdf.Stream (dict, data) -> string_of_stream dict data
  | Pdf.Indirect i -> Printf.sprintf "%i 0 R" i
```

The cases are all simple, except for the ones we have put aside to be implemented separately. Strings must be put between parentheses, indirect references are printed as 2 0 R etc.

To build a string from an `Array`, we need to start with an open square bracket, add the string for each Pdf.pdfobject in the array (which may be arbitrarily complex, of course), and put spaces between them. Then we end with a close square bracket:

Chapter 14. Writing Documents

```
string_of_array : Pdf.pdfobject → string

let rec string_of_array a =
  let b = Buffer.create 100 in
    Buffer.add_string b "[";
    List.iter
      (fun s ->
         Buffer.add_char b ' ';
         Buffer.add_string b (string_of_pdfobject s))
      a;
    Buffer.add_string b " ]";
    Buffer.contents b
```

It is natural to use the **Buffer** module from the Standard Library to collect these strings together. It is also more efficient than using string concatenation. Notice we do not add an initial space after the square bracket, but do before the closing square bracket, for symmetry. The `string_of_dictionary` function is somewhat similar:

```
string_of_dictionary : Pdf.pdfobject → string

let rec string_of_dictionary d =
  let b = Buffer.create 100 in
    Buffer.add_string b "<<";
    List.iter
      (fun (k, v) ->
         Buffer.add_char b ' ';
         Buffer.add_string b k;
         Buffer.add_char b ' ';
         Buffer.add_string b (string_of_pdfobject v))
      d;
    Buffer.add_string b " >>";
    Buffer.contents b
```

Now for `string_of_stream`. A stream in PDF is written like this:

stream dictionary
stream
stream data
endstream

This is simple with the **Buffer** module too:

```
string_of_stream : Pdf.pdfobject → string → string

let rec string_of_stream dict data =
  let b = Buffer.create 100 in
    List.iter (Buffer.add_string b)
      [string_of_pdfobject dict; "\nstream\n"; data; "\nendstream"];
    Buffer.contents b
```

The code for these four functions is collected together in Figure 14.1. Now that we can build a string from any Pdf.pdfobject, we can proceed to build the `write_header`, `write_trailer`, and `write_objects` functions, so that we have everything we need for the final `pdf_to_file` function.

The PDF header consists of %%PDF-$m.n$ where m and n are the major and minor version numbers. This is easy to build with `Printf.sprintf`:

```
write_header : out_channel → Pdf.t → unit

let write_header o {Pdf.version = (major, minor)} =
  output_string o
    (Printf.sprintf "%%PDF-%i.%i\n" major minor)
```

The `write_objects` function, which is given a list of (**int** × Pdf.pdfobject) pairs, sorts the objects by their number, and then outputs each object using `string_of_pdfobject`. For example, the pair

```
(3,
 Dictionary
   [("/Type", Name "/Pages"); ("/Kids", Array [Indirect 1]); ("/Count", Integer 1)])
```

will be written to file like this:

```
3 0 obj
<< /Type /Pages /Kids [1 0 R] /Count 1 >>
endobj
```

The function collects and returns a list of the byte offsets of the objects written, since this will be needed to write the trailer section, which we shall describe in a moment.

```
write_objects : out_channel → (int × Pdf.pdfobject) → int list

let write_objects o objs =
  let offsets = ref [] in
    List.iter
      (fun (objnum, obj) ->
         offsets := pos_out o :: !offsets;
         output_string o (Printf.sprintf "%i 0 obj\n" objnum);
         output_string o (string_of_pdfobject obj);
         output_string o "\nendobj\n")
      (List.sort objs);
    List.rev !offsets
```

Chapter 14. Writing Documents

```
string_of_array : Pdf.pdfobject list → string
string_of_dictionary : (string × Pdf.pdfobject) list → string
string_of_stream : Pdf.pdfobject → string → string
string_of_pdfobject : Pdf.pdfobject → string

let rec string_of_array a =
  let b = Buffer.create 100 in
    Buffer.add_string b "[";
    List.iter
      (fun s ->
         Buffer.add_char b ' ';
         Buffer.add_string b (string_of_pdfobject s))
      a;
    Buffer.add_string b " ]";
    Buffer.contents b

and string_of_dictionary d =
  let b = Buffer.create 100 in
    Buffer.add_string b "<<";
    List.iter
      (fun (k, v) ->
         Buffer.add_char b ' ';
         Buffer.add_string b k;
         Buffer.add_char b ' ';
         Buffer.add_string b (string_of_pdfobject v))
      d;
    Buffer.add_string b " >>";
    Buffer.contents b

and string_of_stream dict data =
  let b = Buffer.create 100 in
    List.iter (Buffer.add_string b)
      [string_of_pdfobject dict; "\nstream\n"; data; "\nendstream"];
    Buffer.contents b

and string_of_pdfobject obj =
  match obj with
    Pdf.Boolean b -> string_of_bool b
  | Pdf.Integer i -> string_of_int i
  | Pdf.Float f -> string_of_float f
  | Pdf.String s -> "(" ^ s ^ ")"
  | Pdf.Name n -> n
  | Pdf.Array a -> string_of_array a
  | Pdf.Dictionary d -> string_of_dictionary d
  | Pdf.Stream (dict, data) -> string_of_stream dict data
  | Pdf.Indirect i -> Printf.sprintf "%i 0 R" i
```

Figure 14.1: Our mutually recursive functions to build a string from a Pdf.pdfobject

Now, we can write the trailer. That is to say, this section:

```
xref
0 5
0000000000 65535 f
0000000015 00000 n
0000000230 00000 n
0000000279 00000 n
0000000338 00000 n
trailer
<< /Size 5 /Root 2 0 R >>
startxref
440
%%EOF
```

This consists largely of a list of the byte offsets of the four objects in the file (15, 230, 279, 338), the trailer dictionary, and so on. It is not necessary to understand it in detail. This is the first section which would be read by a PDF reader, to find the actual objects in the file.

```
write_trailer : out_channel → Pdf.t → int list → unit

let write_trailer o pdf offsets =
  let startxref = pos_out o in
    output_string o "xref\n";
    output_string o
      (Printf.sprintf "0 %i\n" (List.length pdf.Pdf.objects + 1));
    output_string o "0000000000 65535 f \n";
    List.iter
      (fun offset ->
        output_string o (Printf.sprintf "%010i 00000 n \n" offset))
      offsets;
    output_string o "trailer\n";
    output_string o (string_of_pdfobject pdf.Pdf.trailer);
    output_string o "\nstartxref\n";
    output_string o (string_of_int startxref);
    output_string o "\n%%EOF"
```

Now the main function is simple. We open the file, write the header, objects, and trailer, and close the file. In the event of an exception, we close the file to clean up, and re-raise it.

Chapter 14. Writing Documents

```
pdf_to_file : Pdf.t → string → unit

let pdf_to_file pdf filename =
  let output = open_out_bin filename in
    try
      write_header output pdf;
      let offsets = write_objects output pdf.Pdf.objects in
        write_trailer output pdf offsets;
        close_out output
    with
      e -> close_out output; raise e
```

This code goes into `pdfwrite.ml`. The interface `pdfwrite.mli` is very simple. We expose only `pdf_to_file`:

```
val pdf_to_file : Pdf.t -> string -> unit
```

Here is the output of our program on the example Pdfhello.hello:

```
%PDF-1.1
1 0 obj
<< /Type /Page /Parent 3 0 R /Resources << /Font << /F0 << /Type /Font /Subtype /
    Type1 /BaseFont /Times-Italic >> >> >> /MediaBox [ 0. 0. 595.275590551
    841.88976378 ] /Rotate 0 /Contents [ 4 0 R ] >>
endobj
2 0 obj
<< /Type /Catalog /Pages 3 0 R >>
endobj
3 0 obj
<< /Type /Pages /Kids [ 1 0 R ] /Count 1 >>
endobj
4 0 obj
<< /Length 53 >>
stream
1 0 0 1 50 770 cm BT /F0 36 Tf (Hello, World!) Tj ET
endstream
endobj
xref
0 5
0000000000 65535 f
0000000015 00000 n
0000000230 00000 n
0000000279 00000 n
0000000338 00000 n
trailer
<< /Size 5 /Root 2 0 R >>
startxref
```

```
440
%%EOF
```

This loads correctly into a PDF viewer. Notice that some of the spacing is different from the specimen PDF we had at the top of the chapter – this does not matter. Now we can move on to putting more interesting content on the page of our PDF documents.

Chapter 14. Writing Documents

Questions

1. Modify the code so that arrays and dictionaries do not have spaces at either end of them (these spaces are not required). For example, we should see [2 0 R] rather than [2 0 R].

2. Build an example PDF with three pages. This will have three entries in its /Kids array, and three page objects. The page contents may be shared by the three pages if desired. You will need to number the additional objects carefully.

3. Modify the program to use our byte-by-byte compression algorithm from Chapter 6 to compress the content stream in the "Hello, World" program. You will need to fix the /Length and add /Filter /RunLengthDecode to the stream dictionary. Now modify the program to use our bit-by-bit compression algorithm from the same chapter with /Filter /CCITTFaxDecode. You will need to add the following entry to the stream dictionary, in addition to altering the /Filter entry:

```
("/DecodeParms",
   Pdf.Dictionary
     [("/Rows", Pdf.Integer 1);
      ("/Columns", Pdf.Integer (52 * 8));
      ("/BlackIs1", Pdf.Boolean true);
      ("/EndOfBlock", Pdf.Boolean false)])
```

The number 52 is the number of bytes of data in our example.

Chapter 15

Pretty Pictures

We have not yet explained the structure of the code which put "Hello, World!" on the page. Here it is again:

```
1 0 0 1 50 770 cm BT /F0 36 Tf (Hello, World!) Tj ET
```

It is a list of operator-operand sequences. Each sequence consists of zero or more operands and one operator. The sequences in our example are:

Operands	Operator
1 0 0 1 50 770	cm
	BT
/F0 36	Tf
(Hello, World!)	Tj
	ET

In this chapter we will introduce a few simple operators for drawing lines and filling shapes (in the next chapter we discuss adding text and build a basic typesetter). Here are the operators we will be using to start with:

Operands	Operator	Description
x y	m	move to point
x y	l	line to point
	h	close path
	S	stroke path
	f	fill path
0...1	g	set fill grey
0...1	G	set stroke grey

Here is a data type, which forms part of the new Pdfpage module, which encodes these operators. We will extend it with new operators when required.

```
type t =
    Move of float * float
  | Line of float * float
  | Close
  | Stroke
  | Fill
  | FillColour of float
  | StrokeColour of float
```

In order to put these into the PDF document, we will need to convert each set of operands and operator to a string. This is simple:

```
string_of_op : Pdfpage.t → string

let string_of_op op =
  match op with
    Move (x, y) -> Printf.sprintf "%f %f m" x y
  | Line (x, y) -> Printf.sprintf "%f %f l" x y
  | Close -> "h"
  | Stroke -> "S"
  | Fill -> "f"
  | FillColour g -> Printf.sprintf "%f g" g
  | StrokeColour g -> Printf.sprintf "%f G" g
```

Now we can put them together into a single string by using functions from the **Buffer** module, putting a space character after each.

```
string_of_ops : Pdfpage.t list → string

let string_of_ops ops =
  let b = Buffer.create 1000 in
    List.iter
      (fun op ->
        Buffer.add_string b (string_of_op op);
        Buffer.add_char b ' ')
      ops;
    Buffer.contents b
```

Here is a very simple example – we move to (100, 100), make three lines and close the path. Then we use the Fill operator. Coordinates in PDF have the origin at the bottom left of the page.

Chapter 15. Pretty Pictures

```
box : Pdfpage.t list

let box =
  [Pdfpage.Move (100., 100.);
   Pdfpage.Line (100., 200.);
   Pdfpage.Line (200., 200.);
   Pdfpage.Line (200., 100.);
   Pdfpage.Close;
   Pdfpage.Fill]
```

Our page looks like this:

Not all sequences of operators are valid, and our data type makes no checks to ensure our list is correct. This could be solved by building a higher-level data type which would then be flattened down to a list of Pdfpage.t elements. In our examples, and in the questions at the end of the chapter, it is sufficient to stick to the pattern above – one Move, one or more Lines, a Close (if filling), and a Fill or Stroke.

As an example, we will build a function to make a single line, and use it to build a function which, given the page dimensions, draws a page of graph paper. First, a function to build a single line from (x, y) to $(x1, y1)$:

```
mkline : float → float → float → float → Pdfpage.t list

let mkline x y x1 y1 =
  [Pdfpage.Move (x, y);
   Pdfpage.Line (x1, y1);
   Pdfpage.Stroke]
```

Now, a function to return a set of equally spaced floating-point values from $0 \ldots n$ given a step:

```
steps : float → float → float list

let steps n step =
  let mul = ref 0
  and vals = ref [] in
    while float !mul *. step <= n do
      vals := float !mul *. step :: !vals;
      mul := !mul + 1
    done;
    List.rev !vals
```

Note that we have been careful to avoid repeated addition of floating-point values – this can accumulate errors. We can build all the lines:

```
graph_string : float → float → float → string

let graph_string w h step =
  let horizontals =
    List.map (fun n -> mkline 0. n w n) (steps h step)
  and verticals =
    List.map (fun n -> mkline n 0. n h) (steps w step)
  in
    Pdfpage.string_of_ops (List.concat (horizontals @ verticals))
```

Here is the result of `graph_string 595.28 841.89 10.` on a page of A4 paper:

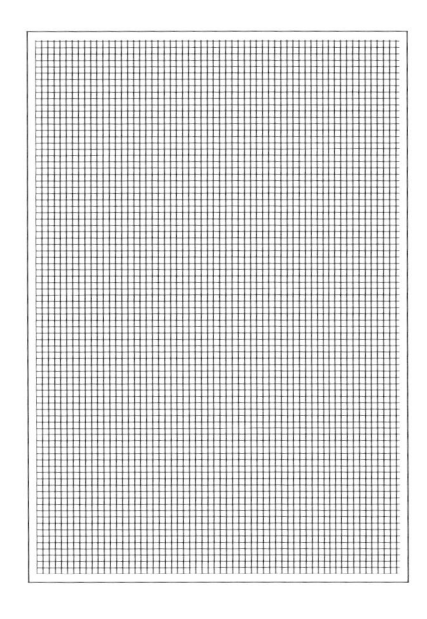

Chapter 15. Pretty Pictures

Questions

1. Write a function which, given a centre point and radius, returns a list of Move, Line, and Close elements which represent a circle. Use a number of lines appropriate to the size of the circle.

2. Use the function from the previous question to write a program which outputs a page covered in pseudo-random sized and filled grey circles.

3. The sequences *red green blue* rg and *red green blue* RG are the colour analogues to the sequences *grey* g and *grey* G. Add them to our data type, and redo the circles program to use colour.

4. The sequence *width* w sets the line width. Add this to our data type and use it to draw a single large unfilled circle over the centre of the page.

5. The operator W in place of a stroke or paint operator is used to set up a *clipping path*. Add this to our data type. Turn your big circle into a clipping path for the random circles pattern, so you now have circles within a circle.

Chapter 16

Adding Text

In this chapter, we will develop a very simple typesetter. Given a string representing the page content, it will split it into words, break them across lines and place them on the page. In the questions at the end of the chapter, the typesetter will be extended to use full justification, to indent paragraphs, and to produce multi-page documents.

To begin with, some of our numbers (lines per page, margins etc.) will be hard coded – we will then factor them out as we generalize the code. But let us define names for the page width and height for an A4 page first, to prevent excessive duplication:

```
page_width : float
page_height : float

let page_width = 595.28

let page_height = 841.89
```

We first need to split our text into words. For our purposes, a word is anything separated from another word by one or more spaces. To preserve the paragraph breaks, the new line character \n will be considered a word also. So, for example, the string "He stopped.\n Looking around, he saw he was enveloped in smoke." would be split into the list of words ["He"; "stopped."; "\n"; "Looking"; "around,"; "he"; "saw"; "he"; "was"; "enveloped"; "in"; "smoke."].

The function consume_spaces, given an input, places the input position at the first non-space character at or after its current position. If the end of the input is reached, no exception is raised.

```
consume_spaces : Input.input → unit

let consume_spaces i =
  try
    while true do
      match i.Input.input_char () with
        ' ' -> ()
      | x -> rewind i; raise End_of_file
    done;
      assert false
  with
    End_of_file -> ()
```

Now we can write a function to read a word. First, we consume any spaces present. Then, we repeatedly read characters into a buffer until either a space occurs, a newline occurs, or we reach the end of a file. If a space occurs, we have finished reading the word. If a newline occurs, we have finished also, but we rewind so the newline will be picked up as its own word next time. If we reach the end of the input, we return the contents of the buffer so far.

```
read_word : Input.input → string

let read_word i =
  consume_spaces i;                                    discard any initial space
  let b = Buffer.create 20 in
    try
      while true do
        match i.Input.input_char () with
          '\n' ->                                      newline
            if Buffer.length b = 0
              then Buffer.add_char b '\n'
              else rewind i;
            raise End_of_file
        | ' ' -> raise End_of_file                     space
        | c -> Buffer.add_char b c                     any other character
      done;
      assert false
    with
      End_of_file ->
        if Buffer.length b = 0                         if we have read nothing…
          then raise End_of_file                       …we have no word, but are at the end…
          else Buffer.contents b                       …otherwise we have a final word
```

Now it is simple to collect all the words in an input by repeatedly calling `read_word`, and accumulating the result is a list.

Chapter 16. Adding Text

```
words_of_input : Input.input → string list

let words_of_input i =
  let words = ref [] in
    try
      while true do words := read_word i :: !words done;
      assert false
    with
      End_of_file -> List.rev !words
```

We shall consider the opening paragraphs of Kafka's "Metamorphosis":

```
One morning, when Gregor Samsa woke from troubled dreams, he found
himself transformed in his bed into a horrible vermin.  He lay on
his armour-like back, and if he lifted his head a little he could
see his brown belly, slightly domed and divided by arches into stiff
sections.  The bedding was hardly able to cover it and seemed ready
to slide off any moment.  His many legs, pitifully thin compared
with the size of the rest of him, waved about helplessly as he
looked.
        "What's happened to me?" he thought. It wasn't a dream. His
room, a proper human room although a little too small, lay peacefully
between its four familiar walls. A collection of textile samples lay
spread out on the table - Samsa was a travelling salesman - and above
it there hung a picture that he had recently cut out of an
illustrated magazine and housed in a nice, gilded frame. It showed a
lady fitted out with a fur hat and fur boa who sat upright, raising a
heavy fur muff that covered the whole of her lower arm towards the
viewer.
```

So, for our text, we get:

```
["One"; "morning,"; "when"; "Gregor"; "Samsa"; "woke"; "from"; "troubled";
 "dreams,"; "he"; "found"; "himself"; "transformed"; "in"; "his"; "bed";
 "into"; "a"; "horrible"; "vermin."; "He"; "lay"; "on"; "his"; "armour-like";
 "back,"; "and"; "if"; "he"; "lifted"; "his"; "head"; "a"; "little"; "he";
 "could"; "see"; "his"; "brown"; "belly,"; "slightly"; "domed"; "and";
 "divided"; "by"; "arches"; "into"; "stiff"; "sections."; "The"; "bedding";
 "was"; "hardly"; "able"; "to"; "cover"; "it"; "and"; "seemed"; "ready";
 "to"; "slide"; "off"; "any"; "moment."; "His"; "many"; "legs,"; "pitifully";
 "thin"; "compared"; "with"; "the"; "size"; "of"; "the"; "rest"; "of";
 "him,"; "waved"; "about"; "helplessly"; "as"; "he"; "looked."; "\n";
 "\"What's"; "happened"; "to"; "me?\""; "he"; "thought."; "It"; ...]
```

Notice the newline as a word on its own. Our next task is to break this sequence of words into lines of a given width. We will have two kinds of line. A `Full` line is one we had to break at the end of. A `Partial` line is one which ended because of a newline or end-of-input. In our first example, we will not need to distinguish these two, but when it comes to justification and more advanced examples, it will be invaluable. The type is trivial:

```
type line =
    Full of string
  | Partial of string
```

Now the line breaking function. The function `lines` takes a maximum width in characters, and a list of words, and returns a line list. There are three cases in the `lines_inner` function:

1. If we have reached the end of the list of words, return the list of collected `lines`, adding one for anything in the current line buffer, if it is non-empty.
2. If we have a newline word, create a `Partial` line from the current buffer (even if it is empty – this allows blank lines to be inserted using multiple newlines), and carry on.
3. If we have any other word, see how long it and the buffer are. If the word is longer than the whole line and we are at the beginning of that line, we output an over-sized line (an alternative would be to wrap or hyphenate the word in some way). Otherwise, we see if the current word will fit. If it will, we add it and a space to the buffer and carry on. It not, we output a `Full` line, and start with the word on the next line.

```
lines_inner : line list → Buffer.t → int → string list → line list
lines : int → string list → line list

let rec lines_inner ls b width words =
  match words with
    [] ->                                                              case 1
      if Buffer.length b > 0 then
        List.rev (Partial (Buffer.contents b) :: ls)
      else
        List.rev ls
  | "\n"::t ->                                                         case 2
      lines_inner
        (Partial (Buffer.contents b) :: ls)
        (Buffer.create width) width t
  | word::t ->                                                         case 3
      if Buffer.length b = 0 && String.length word > width then
        lines_inner (Full word :: ls) (Buffer.create width) width t
      else if String.length word + Buffer.length b < width then
        begin
          Buffer.add_string b word;
          Buffer.add_char b ' ';
          lines_inner ls b width t
        end
      else
        lines_inner
          (Full (Buffer.contents b) :: ls)
          (Buffer.create width) width (word :: t)

let lines width words =
  lines_inner [] (Buffer.create width) width words
```

For example, here is our text split into lines of no more than twenty characters each:

Chapter 16. Adding Text

```
[Text.Full "One morning, when "; Text.Full "Samsa woke from ";
 Text.Full "dreams, he found "; Text.Full "transformed in his ";
 Text.Full "into a horrible "; Text.Full "He lay on his ";
 Text.Full "back, and if he "; Text.Full "his head a little ";
 Text.Full "could see his brown "; Text.Full "slightly domed and ";
 Text.Full "by arches into "; Text.Full "sections. The ";
 Text.Full "was hardly able to "; Text.Full "it and seemed ready ";
 Text.Full "slide off any "; Text.Full "His many legs, ";
 Text.Full "thin compared with "; Text.Full "size of the rest of ";
 Text.Full "waved about "; Text.Partial "as he looked. ";
 Text.Full "\"What's happened to "; Text.Full "he thought. It ";
 Text.Full "a dream. His room, "; Text.Full "proper human room ";
 Text.Full "a little too small, "; Text.Full "peacefully between "; ...]
```

Now we need to add appropriate text-showing operators to our Pdfpage module, and then produce a list of operators for showing a line, using it repeatedly to show the whole page. A text section in a PDF operator stream looks something like this:

```
BT 1 0 0 1 40 50 Tm /F0 12 Tf (The text) Tj ET
```

This contains the following operators and operands:

Operands	Operator	Description
-	BT	begin text section
1 0 0 1 40 50	Tm	move text position to $(40, 50)$
/F0 12	Tf	set font to 12pt /F0
(The Text)	Tj	show the text string "The Text"
-	ET	end text section

Here are the fragments added to the Pdfpage.t type...

```
| BeginText
| EndText
| SetTextPosition of float * float
| SetFontAndSize of string * float
| ShowText of string
```

...and the string_of_op function:

```
| BeginText -> "BT"
| EndText -> "ET"
| SetTextPosition (x, y) -> Printf.sprintf "1 0 0 1 %f %f Tm" x y
| SetFontAndSize (font, size) -> Printf.sprintf "%s %f Tf" font size
| ShowText t -> Printf.sprintf "(%s) Tj" t
```

Consider Figure 16.1. The function typeset_line_at builds a single line at x position 20 and a given y coordinate. The function downfrom builds a list of y positions for a number of lines. The utility function clean_lines makes plain strings from a list of lines, and the function typeset_page puts it all together, generating a big list of Pdfpage.t operations. The resulting PDF is shown in Figure 16.2. The full code for this chapter is included in the online resources – it should be consulted before attempting the questions.

```
typeset_line_at : string → float → Pdfpage.t list
downfrom : float → float → int → int → float list
clean_lines : line list → string list
typeset_page : string → Pdfpage.t list

let typeset_line_at line y =
  [Pdfpage.BeginText;
   Pdfpage.SetTextPosition (20., y);
   Pdfpage.SetFontAndSize ("/F0", 12.0);
   Pdfpage.ShowText line;
   Pdfpage.EndText]

let rec downfrom step start length n =
  if length = 0 then [] else
    start -. (step *. float n) ::
      downfrom step start (length - 1) (n + 1)

let clean_lines =
  List.map (fun Full x -> x | Partial x -> x)

let typeset_page text =
  let words = words_of_input (Input.input_of_string text) in
    let ls = clean_lines (lines 76 words) in
      let positions =
        downfrom 14. (page_height -. 30.)  (List.length ls) 0
    in
      List.concat (List.map2 typeset_line_at ls positions)
```

Figure 16.1

Chapter 16. Adding Text

```
One morning, when Gregor Samsa woke from troubled dreams, he found himself
in his bed into a horrible vermin. He lay on his armour-like back, and if
lifted his head a little he could see his brown belly, slightly domed and
by arches into stiff sections. The bedding was hardly able to cover it and
ready to slide off any moment. His many legs, pitifully thin compared with
size of the rest of him, waved about helplessly as he looked.
"What's happened to me?" he thought. It wasn't a dream. His room, a proper
room although a little too small, lay peacefully between its four familiar
A collection of textile samples lay spread out on the table - Samsa was a
salesman - and above it there hung a picture that he had recently cut out
an illustrated magazine and housed in a nice, gilded frame. It showed a
fitted out with a fur hat and fur boa who sat upright, raising a heavy fur
that covered the whole of her lower arm towards the viewer.
Gregor then turned to look out the window at the dull weather. Drops of
could be heard hitting the pane, which made him feel quite sad. "How about
I sleep a little bit longer and forget all this nonsense", he thought, but
was something he was unable to do because he was used to sleeping on his
and in his present state couldn't get into that position. However hard he
himself onto his right, he always rolled back to where he was. He must have
it a hundred times, shut his eyes so that he wouldn't have to look at the
legs, and only stopped when he began to feel a mild, dull pain there that
had never felt before.
"Oh, God", he thought, "what a strenuous career it is that I've chosen!
day in and day out. Doing business like this takes much more effort than
your own business at home, and on top of that there's the curse of
worries about making train connections, bad and irregular food, contact
different people all the time so that you can never get to know anyone or
friendly with them. It can all go to Hell!" He felt a slight itch up on his
pushed himself slowly up on his back towards the headboard so that he could
his head better; found where the itch was, and saw that it was covered with
of little white spots which he didn't know what to make of; and when he
to feel the place with one of his legs he drew it quickly back because as
as he touched it he was overcome by a cold shudder.
He slid back into his former position. "Getting up early all the time", he
"it makes you stupid. You've got to get enough sleep. Other travelling
live a life of luxury. For instance, whenever I go back to the guest house
the morning to copy out the contract, these gentlemen are always still
there eating their breakfasts. I ought to just try that with my boss; I'd
kicked out on the spot. But who knows, maybe that would be the best thing
me. If I didn't have my parents to think about I'd have given in my notice
long time ago, I'd have gone up to the boss and told him just what I think,
him everything I would, let him know just what I feel. He'd fall right off
desk! And it's a funny sort of business to be sitting up there at your
talking down at your subordinates from up there, especially when you have
go right up close because the boss is hard of hearing. Well, there's still
hope; once I've got the money together to pay off my parents' debt to him -
five or six years I suppose - that's definitely what I'll do. That's when
make the big change. First of all though, I've got to get up, my train
at five."
```

Figure 16.2

Questions

1. Factor out the font size, line height, margin height and automatically calculate the number of characters in a line (the number of characters in a line can be calculated by the formula $5w/3f$ where w is the width of a line and f is the font size). The program should now work for any page size.

2. The first line of each paragraph (save for the first) should be indented by eight characters. Implement this.

3. Implement full justification. This gives a clean left and right margin except for the left margin of the first line in a paragraph and the right margin of the last line of a paragraph. This can be done by altering the spacing between characters and words. Of course, `Partial` lines should not be stretched.

4. Allow the program to generate multiple pages, should the length of the text demand it. This can be done by extending the `/Kids` entry in the PDF file, and producing multiple page objects.

Answers to Questions

Hints may be found on page 189.

Chapter 1 (Unravelling "Fold")

1

This can be achieved by folding the subtraction operator over the deductions, with the starting accumulator set to the budget:

```
deduct : int → int list → int

let deduct budget expenses =
  List.fold_left ( - ) budget expenses

let deduct = List.fold_left ( - )
```

Partial application can be used, as in the second definition.

2

We can use an accumulator starting at zero, and increment it once for each element processed:

```
length : α list → int

let length l =
  List.fold_left (fun a _ -> a + 1) 0 l
```

Since we ignore the element itself, the function is polymorphic.

3

If the list is empty, we return `None`, otherwise we use a left fold which simply replaces the accumulator with each successive element from the list. We must initialize the accumulator, so we pick the first element for that (we have already eliminated the case where there are no elements, so `List.hd` will succeed).

```
last : α list → α option

let last l =
  match l with
    [] -> None
  | _ -> Some (List.fold_left (fun _ e -> e) (List.hd l) l)
```

Not quite idiomatic.

4

If we start from the left, consing each element to the accumulator (which is initially the empty list), the list will be reversed.

```
rev : α list → α list

let rev l =
  List.fold_left (fun a e -> e :: a) [] l
```

Since the accumulator is the empty list (which has type α list), the function remains polymorphic, having the type we would expect.

5

The accumulator begins set to `false`. For each element, we calculate the logical OR of the element tested for equality and the accumulator. If at least one `true` occurs, the result will be `true`.

```
member : α → α list → bool

let member x l =
  List.fold_left (fun a e -> e = x || a) false l
```

Note that this is less efficient than `List.mem` because there is no early exit – the whole list is processed in every case.

6

This is a classic problem. We either need to

- add a space after each word except for the last; or
- add a space before each word except for the first.

With `fold_left` we can detect when we are at the first word, by inspecting the accumulator, and use the second method.

```
sentence : string list → string

let sentence words =
  List.fold_left
    (fun a e -> if a = "" then e else a ^ " " ^ e)
    ""
    words
```

Note that the requirement that the words be non-empty is important here. The efficiency is poor, however, since each string concatenation builds a new string. The Standard Library **Buffer** module is a better approach here.

7

We can use the built-in max function to update the accumulator.

```
max_depth : α tree → int

let max_depth l =
  List.fold_tree (fun _ l r -> 1 + max l r) 0 l
```

The current element is ignored.

8

We can compare the speed of List.mem and member with the help of the Unix.gettimeofday function, as shown in Figure A.1. On the Author's machine, this results in:

```
Our member took 2.513232 seconds
List.mem took 1.162159 seconds
```

There is a significant speed penalty in our version of the member function, at least for this scenario.

Chapter 2 (Being Lazy)

1

This is similar to the lseq function in the text, but we double every time instead of adding one.

```
ldouble : int → int lazylist
thedoubles : int lazylist

let rec ldouble n =
  Cons (n, fun () -> ldouble (n * 2))

let thedoubles = ldouble 1
```

```
l   : int list
t   : float
t'  : float
t'' : float

let l = [1; 2; 3; 2; 1; 2; 2; 56; 32; 2; 34; 4; 2]

let t = Unix.gettimeofday ()

let _ =
  for x = 1 to 10_000_000 do ignore (member 56 l) done

let t' = Unix.gettimeofday ()

let _ =
  for x = 1 to 10_000_000 do ignore (List.mem 56 l) done

let t'' = Unix.gettimeofday ()

let _ =
  Printf.printf "Our member took %f seconds\n" (t' -. t);
  Printf.printf "List.mem took %f seconds\n" (t'' -. t')
```

Figure A.1

Having written the function which, given a number, doubles from that point, we then just code the list itself by starting at 1.

2

If we are asked to fetch the 0th element, we already have it – as the head of the lazy list. If not, we force evaluation of the tail, and recurse.

```
lnth : α lazylist → int → α

let rec lnth (Cons (h, tf)) n =
  match n with
    0 -> h
  | _ -> lnth (tf ()) (n - 1)
```

Of course, this does not terminate on bad inputs (when $n < 0$). Error detection should be added.

3

Below, the function lrepeating_inner takes the current list c and the original list l. Matching on c, we build the lazy list. If we reach the last element of the input list, we start again, with the original list, which is always retained.

Answers to Questions

```
lrepeating_inner : α list → α list → α lazylist
lrepeating : α tree → α lazylist

let rec lrepeating_inner c l =
  match c with
    [] -> raise (Invalid_argument "lrepeating: empty list")
  | [x] -> Cons (x, fun () -> lrepeating_inner l l)
  | h::t -> Cons (h, fun () -> lrepeating_inner t l)

let lrepeating l = lrepeating_inner l l
```

Note that we cannot build from an empty list, since there could be no head.

4

The first two fibonacci numbers are defined to be 0 and 1. Thereafter, we keep the current and previous number, and generate the lazy list.

```
fibonacci_inner : int → int → int lazylist
fibonacci : int lazylist

let rec fibonacci_inner x y =
  Cons (x, fun () -> fibonacci_inner y (x + y))

let fibonacci = fibonacci_inner 0 1
```

5

This is slightly delicate. We must force the tail twice, to reveal new elements for the heads of the two output lists, and the final tail for the next time each list is forced.

```
unleave : α lazylist → α lazylist × α lazylist

let rec unleave (Cons (h, tf)) =
  let Cons (h', tf') = tf () in
    let t = tf' () in
      (Cons (h, fun () -> fst (unleave t)),
       Cons (h', fun () -> snd (unleave t)))
```

Note that we cannot hoist the calculation of `unleave t` into a **let** so as to do it once, since to do so would not delay evaluation.

6

If we write a function which, given a number, gives the correct string, then the lazy list itself is easy to build with lmap and lseq.

```
letter_string : int → string
alphas : string lazylist

let rec letter_string n =
  if n <= 26 then
    Char.escaped (char_of_int (n + 64))
  else
    letter_string ((n - 1) / 26) ^
    letter_string (((n - 1) mod 26) + 1)

let alphas =
  lmap letter_string (lseq 1)
```

Chapter 3 (Named Tuples with Records)

1

Since a reference is just a record with a mutable field contents, we can use the <- construct:

OCaml

```
# let x = ref 0;;
val x : int ref = {contents = 0}
# x.contents <- 1;;
- : unit = ()
# x;;
- : int ref = {contents = 1}
```

There is no reason to use this rather than := of course.

2

The function Unix.time returns the current time. The function Unix.localtime builds from this a record of type **Unix.tm**. First we will need two ancillary functions:

```
string_of_month : int → string
string_of_day : int → string

let string_of_month m =
  match m with
    0 -> "January"
  | 1 -> "February"
  | 2 -> "March"
  | 3 -> "April"
  | 4 -> "May"
  | 5 -> "June"
  | 6 -> "July"
  | 7 -> "August"
  | 8 -> "September"
  | 9 -> "October"
  | 10 -> "November"
  | 11 -> "December"
  | _ -> raise (Invalid_argument "string_of_month")

let string_of_day d =
  match d with
    0 -> "Sunday"
  | 1 -> "Monday"
  | 2 -> "Tuesday"
  | 3 -> "Wednesday"
  | 4 -> "Thursday"
  | 5 -> "Friday"
  | 6 -> "Saturday"
  | _ -> raise (Invalid_argument "string_of_day")
```

Now the main function, which both uses the shortened form of a record pattern, and names only the fields we need:

```
print_time : unit → unit

let string_of_time () =
  let
    {Unix.tm_min;
     Unix.tm_hour;
     Unix.tm_mday;
     Unix.tm_mon;
     Unix.tm_year;
     Unix.tm_wday}
  =
    Unix.localtime (Unix.time ())
  in
    "It is "
    ^ string_of_int tm_hour
    ^ ":"
    ^ string_of_int tm_min
    ^ " on "
    ^ string_of_day tm_wday
    ^ " "
    ^ string_of_int tm_mday
    ^ " "
    ^ string_of_month tm_mon
    ^ " "
    ^ string_of_int (tm_year + 1900)
```

Note that the names bound by the pattern do not include the Unix prefix.

3

The construct **type** t = {x : int ref} is a record type containing a reference to an integer. We can build it using an existing reference, and can extract the reference for use elsewhere. We can share a single reference between two or more instances of this data type. The construct **type** t = {**mutable** x : int} is a record with a single, mutable field. We must use <- rather than := to mutate it, and it may not be shared.

4

We can use multiple type parameters (which are written with parentheses and commas) and then use these types for the fields in the appropriate way:

```
type ('a, 'b, 'c) t =
  {a : 'a;
   b : 'a;
   c : 'b;
   d : 'b;
   e : 'c;
   f : 'c}
```

5

For the first part, we can use the function Gc.stat to return a **Gc.stat** record. Then we can write various components to the given file (here, we have chosen just a few):

```
write_gc_summary : string → unit

let write_gc_summary filename =
  let ch = open_out filename in
    let
      {Gc.minor_words;
       Gc.promoted_words;
       Gc.major_words;
       Gc.minor_collections;
       Gc.major_collections}
    =
      Gc.stat ()
    in
      output_string ch "Minor Words: ";
      output_string ch (string_of_float minor_words);
      output_string ch "\nPromoted Words: ";
      output_string ch (string_of_float promoted_words);
      output_string ch "\nMajor Words: ";
      output_string ch (string_of_float major_words);
      output_string ch "\nMinor Collections: ";
      output_string ch (string_of_int minor_collections);
      output_string ch "\nMajor Collections: ";
      output_string ch (string_of_int major_collections);
      close_out ch
```

For the second part, we define names for the magic numbers given in the documentation. We can then write a function change_verbosity which adds them up to make the new flags field, and uses Gc.get together with the **with** syntax to build a new record to be passed to Gc.set:

```
start_of_major : int
minor_collection : int
heap_grow_shrink : int
stack_resizing : int
heap_compaction : int
change_parameters : int
compute_slice_size : int
call_finalisation : int
bytecode_exe_search : int
change_verbosity : int list → unit

let start_of_major = 0x001
let minor_collection = 0x002
let heap_grow_shrink = 0x004
let stack_resizing = 0x008
let heap_compaction = 0x010
let change_parameters = 0x020
let compute_slice_size = 0x040
let call_finalisation = 0x080
let bytecode_exe_search = 0x100

let change_verbosity vs =
  let n = List.fold_left ( + ) 0 vs in
    Gc.set {(Gc.get ()) with Gc.verbose = n}
```

Chapter 4 (Generalized Input/Output)

1

This is a simple modification of `input_of_string` from the text, replacing string operators with array ones.

```
input_of_array : char array → input

let input_of_array a =
  let pos = ref 0 in
    {pos_in = (fun () -> !pos);
     seek_in =
       (fun p ->
          if p < 0 then raise (Invalid_argument "seek < 0");
            pos := p);
     input_char =
       (fun () ->
          if !pos > Array.length a - 1
            then raise End_of_file
            else (let c = a.(!pos) in pos := !pos + 1; c));
     in_channel_length = Array.length a}
```

Note that an array of characters like this requires much more space as a string.

2

We create a **Buffer.t**, attempt to read the specified number of characters, and then return the contents. If one of the calls to `i.input_char ()` raises the `End_of_file` exception, we return the buffer contents anyway – it will contain the characters read so far.

```
input_string : input → int → string

let input_string i n =
  let b = Buffer.create 100 in
    try
      for x = 0 to n - 1 do
        Buffer.add_char b (i.input_char ())
      done;
      Buffer.contents b
    with
      End_of_file -> Buffer.contents b
```

3

We add a function of the expected type to the input. The option **None** will represent the end of the file.

```
type input =
  {pos_in : unit -> int;
   seek_in : int -> unit;
   input_char : unit -> char;
   input_char_opt : unit -> char option;
   in_channel_length : int}
```

Now for a new `input_of_channel`. We try to build the `Some` option, returning `None` if the `End_of_file` exception is raised.

```
input_of_channel : in_channel → input

let input_of_channel ch =
  {pos_in = (fun () -> pos_in ch);
   seek_in = seek_in ch;
   input_char = (fun () -> input_char ch);
   input_char_opt =
     (fun () ->
        try Some (input_char ch) with End_of_file -> None);
   in_channel_length = in_channel_length ch}
```

The `input_of_string` function is another similar modification. This time, there is no need for exception handling.

```
input_of_string : string → input

let input_of_string s =
  let pos = ref 0 in
    {pos_in = (fun () -> !pos);
     seek_in =
       (fun p ->
          if p < 0 then raise (Invalid_argument "seek < 0");
          pos := p);
     input_char =
       (fun () ->
          if !pos > String.length s - 1
            then raise End_of_file
            else (let c = s.[!pos] in pos := !pos + 1; c));
     input_char_opt =
       (fun () ->
          if !pos > String.length s - 1
            then None
            else (let c = s.[!pos] in pos := !pos + 1; Some c));
     in_channel_length = String.length s}
```

4

We add the function of type **unit → int**.

```
type input =
  {pos_in : unit -> int;
   seek_in : int -> unit;
   input_char : unit -> char;
   input_byte : unit -> int;
   in_channel_length : int}
```

Now, having defined as a convenience, the name `no_more` for the −1, we can modify `input_of_channel` and `input_of_string` easily:

Answers to Questions

```
no_more : int
input_of_channel : in_channel → input
input_of_string : string → input

let no_more = (-1)

let input_of_channel ch =
  {pos_in = (fun () -> pos_in ch);
   seek_in = seek_in ch;
   input_char = (fun () -> input_char ch);
   input_byte =
     (fun () ->
        try int_of_char (input_char ch) with End_of_file -> no_more);
   in_channel_length = in_channel_length ch}

let input_of_string s =
  let pos = ref 0 in
    {pos_in = (fun () -> !pos);
     seek_in =
       (fun p ->
          if p < 0 then raise (Invalid_argument "seek < 0");
          pos := p);
     input_char =
       (fun () ->
          if !pos > String.length s - 1
            then raise End_of_file
            else (let c = s.[!pos] in pos := !pos + 1; c));
     input_byte =
       (fun () ->
          if !pos > String.length s - 1
            then no_more
            else
              (let c = s.[!pos] in pos := !pos + 1; int_of_char c));
     in_channel_length = String.length s}
```

These functions have none of the advantages of the exception-raising or option-returning ones, but they are very fast indeed.

5

We alter `input_of_channel` to check for a newline and raise `End_of_file` in that case.

```
single_line_input_of_channel : in_channel → input

let single_line_input_of_channel ch =
  {pos_in = (fun () -> pos_in ch);
   seek_in = seek_in ch;
   input_char =
     (fun () ->
       match input_char ch with '\n' -> raise End_of_file | c -> c);
   in_channel_length = in_channel_length ch}
```

Now we can create one of these special inputs from standard input, and use our `input_string` function to build a string from the user's input, ending when the return key is pressed. For example:

```
# input_string (single_line_input_of_channel stdin) max_int;;
Some input
- : string = "Some input"
```

6

Ideal functions to use when defining the new type already exist in the **Buffer** module. Then, we can build an example, where we give a name to the buffer, build an input from it and process it, retrieving its contents afterwards.

```
output_of_buffer : Buffer.t → output
build_buffer : unit → string

let output_of_buffer b =
  {output_char = Buffer.add_char b;
   out_channel_length = fun () -> Buffer.length b}

let build_buffer () =
  let b = Buffer.create 20 in
    let o = output_of_buffer b in
      o.output_char 'A';
      o.output_char 'B';
      o.output_char 'C';
      Buffer.contents b
```

Chapter 5 (Streams of Bits)

1

We can read quickly if the number of bits wanted is 8 and we happen to be at the beginning of a byte. In this case we can call the underlying output's `input_char` function directly.

```
getval_fast : input_bits → int → int

let getval_fast b n =
  if n = 8 && b.bit = 0
    then b.input.input_char ()
    else getval b n
```

If the conditions are not met, we fall back to the old `getval` function. This will be faster if we frequently read data aligned-byte-by-aligned-byte, but we still need the flexibility of a stream of bits when required.

2

We simply replace the **int** operators with those for **Int32.t**:

```
getval_32 : input_bits → int → Int32.t

let getval_32 b n =
  if n < 0 then raise (Invalid_argument "getval_32") else
    if n = 0 then 0l else
      let r = ref Int32.zero in
        for x = n - 1 downto 0 do
          let num = Int32.of_int (if getbit b then 1 else 0) in
            r := Int32.logor !r (Int32.shift_left num x)
        done;
        !r
```

3

Our precondition this time is that the number of bits to be written is 8 and the `obit` field is set to its initial value, 7. Then we can use the `output_char` function of the underlying output.

```
putval_fast : output_bits → int → int → unit

let putval_fast o v l =
  if l = 8 && o.obit = 7
    then o.output.output_char v
    else putval o v l
```

Otherwise, we fall back to the old `putval` function.

4

The integer functions are replaced by ones from the **Int32** module:

```
putval_32 : output_bits → Int32.t → int → unit

let putval_32 o v l =
  for x = l - 1 downto 0 do
    putbit o
      (Int32.to_int
         (Int32.logand v (Int32.shift_left (Int32.of_int x) 1)))
  done
```

5

We add a field `rewind` which will move the position in the output backwards one byte, if possible. This is the new type:

```
type output =
  {output_char : char -> unit;
   rewind : unit -> unit;
   out_channel_length : unit -> int}
```

Now we can rewrite, for example, `output_of_bytes` for this new type:

```
output_of_bytes : bytes → output

let output_of_bytes b =
  let pos = ref 0 in
    {output_char =
       (fun c ->
          if !pos < Bytes.length b
            then (Bytes.set b !pos c; pos := !pos + 1)
            else raise End_of_file);
     rewind =
       (fun () ->
          if !pos > 0
            then pos := !pos - 1
            else raise (Failure "rewind"));
     out_channel_length =
       (fun () -> Bytes.length b)}
```

We alter `putbit` appropriately:

```
putbit : output_bits → int → unit

let rec putbit o b =
  if o.obit = (-1) then
    begin
      o.obyte <- 0;
      o.obit <- 7;
      putbit o b
    end
  else
    begin
      if b <> 0 then o.obyte <- o.obyte lor (1 lsl o.obit);
      o.output.output_char (char_of_int o.obyte);
      o.output.rewind ();
      o.obit <- o.obit - 1
    end
```

Chapter 6 (Compressing Data)

1

We will need to look through the input list of integers (bytes), finding same and different runs and building a new list. For clarity, we will produce the output runs using a new type, producing the actual bytes later:

type run = Same **of** int * int | Diff **of** int list

The Same case holds a (length, value) pair and Diff just a list of bytes. Now we can write a function get_same which, given the first value, the current count, and the list, returns a pair of the final count of like characters, and the remaining list:

```
get_same : α → int → α list → int × α list

let rec get_same x n l =
  match l with
    h::t when h = x -> get_same x (n + 1) t
  | _ -> (n, l)
```

Similarly, we can define a function to read a different run into an accumulator, returning the run and the remaining list. This function will be called only when get_same returned a run of length one.

```
get_different : α → α list → α list × α list

let rec get_different a l =
  match l with
    [] -> (List.rev a, [])
  | h::t ->
      if a = [] then get_different [h] t
      else if h <> List.hd a then get_different (h :: a) t
      else (List.rev (List.tl a), List.hd a :: l)
```

Now we can write a function which uses both of these functions to get a single run, creating an instance of our new data type:

```
getrun : int list → run × int list

let getrun l =
  match l with
    [] -> raise (Invalid_argument "getrun")
  | h::_ ->
    match get_same h 0 l with
      1, _ ->
        let diff, rest = get_different [] l in (Diff diff, rest)
    | n, rest -> (Same (n, h), rest)
```

Now, we use the defined rules to build a function which makes a list of bytes from a run:

```
chars_of_run : run → int list

let chars_of_run r =
  match r with
    Same (length, c) -> [257 - length; c]
  | Diff chars -> List.length chars - 1 :: chars
```

With all this done, it is easy to define the compression function itself, which accumulates runs, concatenating them when all the data has been processed. We must be sure to add the EOD marker at the end.

```
compress_inner : run list → int list → int list
compress : int list → int list

let rec compress_inner a l =
  match l with
    [] -> List.concat (List.map chars_of_run (List.rev a))
  | _ ->
    let run, rest = getrun l in
      compress_inner (run :: a) rest

let compress l = compress_inner [] l @ [128]
```

Decompression is rather simpler, making use of our take and drop functions from the Util module described on page xiii. We read each run and expand it to a list of bytes, accumulating them until end of data.

```
decompress_inner : int list list → int list → int list
decompress : int list → int list

let rec decompress_inner a l =
  match l with
    [128] -> List.concat (List.rev a)
  | [] | [_] -> raise (Invalid_argument "decompress_inner")
  | h::t::t' ->
    if h < 127 then
      let bytes = Util.take (t :: t') (h + 1) in
      let rest = Util.drop (t :: t') (h + 1) in
        decompress_inner (bytes :: a) rest
    else if h > 128 then
      decompress_inner
        (Array.to_list (Array.make (257 - h) t) :: a) t'
    else decompress_inner a []

let decompress l = decompress_inner [] l
```

Note a little cheat – we use functions from the **Array** module to expand the Same run.

2

The tree carries no information in its branches (since no code can be a prefix of another code). Leaves can carry or not carry information, depending on whether there is a code there. In order to avoid **option** types, we can just split into three cases, Lf for empty leaves, Code for full ones, and Br for a branch, where 0 goes left and 1 goes right.

type tree = Lf | Code **of** int | Br **of** tree * tree

Now, we can define the function to add a code to an existing tree. For example, add_elt Lf ([0; 1],

67) adds the code [0; 1] for the run length 67. This will build the tree Br (Br (Lf, Code 67), Lf). We match on the code, building the tree as we go left or right.

```
add_elt : tree → int list × int → tree

let rec add_elt tr (l, n) =
  match l with
    0::m ->
      begin match tr with
        Lf -> Br (add_elt Lf (m, n), Lf)
      | Br (left, right) -> Br (add_elt left (m, n), right)
      | Code x -> raise (Failure "collision")
      end
  | 1::m ->
      begin match tr with
        Lf -> Br (Lf, add_elt Lf (m, n))
      | Br (left, right) -> Br (left, add_elt right (m, n))
      | Code x -> raise (Failure "collision")
      end
  | [] -> Code n
  | _ -> raise (Failure "bad code")
```

Now, to build the whole tree, we just use repeated insertion with fold_left, having built the (code, run length) pairs:

```
make_tree : int list array → int list → tree

let make_tree arr numbers =
  List.fold_left
    add_elt
    Lf
    (List.combine (Array.to_list arr) numbers)
```

Now, for example, we can build the white terminating codes as a tree:

```
white_terminating_tree : tree

let white_terminating_tree =
  make_tree
    white_terminating_codes
    (Util.from 0 (Array.length white_terminating_codes - 1))
```

(Util.from a b gives the list of numbers starting at a and ending at b in ascending order). The function succeeds, verifying that there are no collisions, and yields:

```
    Br
     (Br
       (Br
         (Br
           (Br
             (Br (Br (Lf, Br (Code 29, Code 30)),
                 Br (Br (Code 45, Code 46), Code 22)),
              Br (Br (Code 23, Br (Code 47, Code 48)), Code 13)),
            Br
             (Br (Br (Code 20, Br (Code 33, Code 34)),
                 Br (Br (Code 35, Code 36), Br (Code 37, Code 38))),
              Br (Br (Code 19, Br (Code 31, Code 32)), Code 1))),
          Br
           (Br (Br (Code 12, Br (Br (Code 53, Code 54), Code 26)),
               Br (Br (Br (Code 39, Code 40), Br (Code 41, Code 42)),
                Br (Br (Code 43, Code 44), Code 21))),
            Br
             (Br (Br (Code 28, Br (Code 61, Code 62)),
                 Br (Br (Code 63, Code 0), Lf)),
              Code 10))),
        Br
         (Br
           (Br (Code 11,
               Br (Br (Code 27, Br (Code 59, Code 60)), Br (Lf, Code 18))),
            Br
             (Br (Br (Code 24, Br (Code 49, Code 50)),
                 Br (Br (Code 51, Code 52), Code 25)),
              Br (Br (Br (Code 55, Code 56), Br (Code 57, Code 58)), Lf))),
          Br (Lf, Code 2))),
      Br
       (Br (Br (Code 3, Br (Lf, Code 8)),
           Br (Br (Code 9, Br (Code 16, Code 17)), Code 4)),
        Br (Br (Code 5, Br (Br (Code 14, Code 15), Lf)), Br (Code 6, Code 7))))
```

3

Compressing our data with compress_string input_data 1680 1 instead of compress_string input_data 80 21 generates a string of length 110 bytes rather than 120 bytes. This is because we could generate one run for the white section at the end of one line followed by a white section at the beginning of the next, instead of splitting at line boundaries.

If we try to re-compress this data, with compress_string compressed 880 1, the data size increases to 197 bytes. This is unsurprising, since the job of the white and black codes is to be information-dense and the compression algorithm works best on data which is information-sparse.

4

We can re-use the read_up_to function to build our histogram. Given white and black arrays, each of length 1792 and with elements initialized to zero, the input bits and the width and height, we can repeatedly call read_up_to. We must maintain a count of how many pixels are left to be read, and an additional count of how many are left in this line, so the correct width can be passed to the read_up_to function.

```
build_histogram : int array → int array → input_bits → int → int → unit

let build_histogram a_white a_black i w h =
  let toread = ref (w * h) in
  let wleft = ref w in
    while !toread > 0 do
      let n, v = read_up_to (peekbit i) i 0 !wleft in
        let a = if v then a_black else a_white in
          a.(n) <- a.(n) + 1;
          toread := !toread - n;
          wleft := !wleft - n;
          if !wleft = 0 then wleft := w
    done
```

Now it is easy to build two histograms – one for white and one for black, and return them:

```
histogram_of_input : input → int → int → (int array × int array)

let histogram_of_input i w h =
  let white = Array.make 1792 0 in
    let black = Array.make 1792 0 in
      build_histogram white black (input_bits_of_input i) w h;
      (white, black)
```

We can define a simple function to print the histogram, eliding any zero counts:

```
print_histogram : int array → unit

let print_histogram =
  Array.iteri
    (fun x n ->
      if n > 0 then Printf.printf "%i runs of length %i\n" n x)
```

Here is the histogram for white runs on our example data:

```
# print_histogram white;;
5 runs of length 1
7 runs of length 2
15 runs of length 3
15 runs of length 4
34 runs of length 5
20 runs of length 6
4 runs of length 7
```

```
4 runs of length 8
4 runs of length 9
3 runs of length 10
3 runs of length 11
7 runs of length 12
1 runs of length 13
1 runs of length 14
1 runs of length 15
3 runs of length 16
1 runs of length 17
1 runs of length 20
1 runs of length 21
3 runs of length 35
1 runs of length 39
1 runs of length 46
1 runs of length 47
1 runs of length 73
3 runs of length 80
- : unit = ()
```

And here is the histogram for black runs:

```
# print_histogram black;;
12 runs of length 1
55 runs of length 2
38 runs of length 3
5 runs of length 4
2 runs of length 5
1 runs of length 6
1 runs of length 7
1 runs of length 8
2 runs of length 9
2 runs of length 10
- : unit = ()
```

Chapter 7 (Labelled and Optional Arguments)

1

If α is **int** then the first and second argument can be confused. We can fix this by adding labels and calling `Array.make`. Notice the use of punning here.

```
map : len:int → elt:α → α array

let make ~len ~elt =
  Array.make len elt
```

Now the function can be called without confusion:

```
              OCaml
# make ~len:5 ~elt:4;;
- : int array = [|4; 4; 4; 4; 4|]
```

Of course, it can still be called without labels.

2

We can define separate types for the start and length so that their names must be mentioned when calling the function.

```
fill : α array → start → length → α → unit
filled : unit → string array

type start = Start of int

type length = Length of int

let fill a (Start s) (Length l) v =
  for x = s to s + l - 1 do a.(x) <- v done

let filled () =
  let a = Array.make 100 "x" in
    fill a (Start 20) (Length 40) "y";
    a
```

Not nearly as convenient as labels, though.

3

There are three functions where confusion may arise, and we can label them with simple wrappers. They are the functions where multiple arguments have the same type, and so may be confused.

```
sub : Buffer.t → off:int → len:int → string
blit : Buffer.t → srcoff:int → string → dstoff:int → len:int → unit
add_substring : Buffer.t → string → ofs:int → len:int → unit

let sub b ~off ~len =
  Buffer.sub b off len

let blit src ~srcoff dst ~dstoff ~len =
  Buffer.blit src srcoff dst dstoff len

let add_substring b s ~ofs ~len =
  Buffer.add_substring b s ofs len
```

4

We can make the accumulator an optional argument. Now the caller can call the function as if it were the same as `List.map`.

```
map : ?a:α list → (β → α) → β list → α list

let rec map ?(a = []) f l =
  match l with
    [] -> List.rev a
  | h::t -> map ~a:(f h :: a) f t
```

The optional argument must still appear in the interface, of course, so we might still prefer the old approach of wrapping it up and only exposing the wrapper.

Chapter 8 (Formatted Printing)

1

We can use `Printf.bprintf` to accumulate the individual parts, making sure to deal with the final element specially. The outer function sets everything up.

```
cycle_of_points_inner : Buffer.t → (int × int) list → string
cycle_of_points : (int × int) list → string

let rec cycle_of_points_inner b l =
  match l with
    [] ->
      Buffer.contents b
  | [(x, y)] ->
      Printf.bprintf b "(%i, %i)" x y;
      Buffer.contents b
  | (x, y)::t ->
      Printf.bprintf b "(%i, %i) --> " x y;
      cycle_of_points_inner b t

let cycle_of_points l =
  match l with
    [] -> ""
  | h::t ->
      cycle_of_points_inner (Buffer.create 256) (h :: t @ [h])
```

2

Again, `Printf.bprintf` is the key. This time, we can calculate the initial buffer size exactly.

`hex_of_string` : **string** → **string**

```
let hex_of_string s =
  let b = Buffer.create (String.length s * 2) in
    String.iter
      (fun c -> Printf.bprintf b "%02X" (int_of_char c))
      s;
    Buffer.contents b
```

We have used a width specifier of 2 and the 0 flag to make sure that characters with code 0..15 are padded with a zero.

3

The format string for `Printf.printf` must be known at compile time. The solution for printing the result of `mkstring` using `printf` is the %s format specification:

```
Printf.printf "%s" (mkstring ())
```

4

The * character can be used as a width or precision specifier, to indicate that the width or precision is given as an argument. We use * for the width, and pass in 10.

```
Printf.sprintf "(%*i)" 10 1
```

So, the result is:

```
(         1)
```

We can use `List.iter` to print a table by applying this to each of a list of numbers in turn.

`print_integers` : **int** → **int list** → **unit**

```
let print_integers w ns =
  List.iter (Printf.printf "(%*i)" w) ns
```

Chapter 9 (Searching for Things)

1

For the first part, where all matches are considered, we can rewrite `search` with an extra argument to count the matches, restructuring its logic so as not to finish upon the first match.

```
string' : int → int → string → string → int
string  : string → string → int

let rec search' matches n ss s =
  if String.length ss > String.length s - n then matches else
    if at ss 0 s n (String.length ss)
      then search' (matches + 1) (n + 1) ss s
      else search' matches (n + 1) ss s

let search = search' 0 0
```

There is no need to rewrite the `at` function. Now, for the version which considers only non-overlapping matches, we just jump by the length of the pattern `ss` upon a match:

```
string' : int → int → string → string → int
string  : string → string → int

let rec search' matches n ss s =
  if String.length ss > String.length s - n then matches else
    if at ss 0 s n (String.length ss)
      then search' (matches + 1) (n + String.length ss) ss s
      else search' matches (n + 1) ss s

let search = search' 0 0
```

2

It is simple to write a function which returns the length of the longest matching prefix at the beginning of a list:

```
prefix : α list → α list → int

let rec prefix p l =
  match p, l with
    ph::pt, lh::lt -> if ph = lh then 1 + prefix pt lt else 0
  | _ -> 0
```

Now, we can write a function which keeps track of the position and length of the longest prefix found, returning them when the whole list has been searched.

```
longest_prefix_inner : int → int → int → α list → α list → int × int
longest_prefix : α list → α list → int × int

let rec longest_prefix_inner currpos bestpos bestlen p l =
  match l with
    [] -> (bestpos, bestlen)
  | h::t ->
      let prelen = prefix p l in
        if prelen > bestlen then
          longest_prefix_inner (currpos + 1) currpos prelen p t
        else
          longest_prefix_inner (currpos + 1) bestpos bestlen p t

let longest_prefix p l =
  longest_prefix_inner 0 0 0 p l
```

Here, `currpos` is the current position, `bestpos` the position of the longest matching prefix found so far, and `bestlen` the length of the longest prefix so far.

3

We can write a simple profiling function which, given a search function, measures its running time. This allows us to compare the naive and better versions of `search` we wrote for searching in strings:

```
profile : (string → string → α) → float

let profile f =
  let t = Unix.gettimeofday () in
    for x = 1 to 1_000_000 do
      ignore (f "ABA" "Somewhere in here is the pattern ABBBBAABA.")
    done;
    Unix.gettimeofday () -. t
```

Compiling with `ocamlc` on the Author's machine:

```
Naive version took 7.608291 seconds
Better version tool 3.388830 seconds
```

Now, compiling with `ocamlopt`:

Answers to Questions

```
Naive version took 2.966211 seconds
Better version tool 0.450546 seconds
```

4

We can add a case to the main search. We must check the character following the backslash for a match, assuming there is such a next character. If so, we move two positions in the pattern and one in the string. Otherwise, the match has failed.

```
| '\\' ->
    if
      sp < String.length s &&
      ssp < String.length ss - 1 &&
      ss.[ssp + 1] = s.[sp]
    then
      Some (2, 1)
    else
      None
```

5

The Standard Library function `String.uppercase` can be used, in conjunction with the optional boolean argument:

---

search : ?nocase:**bool** → **string** → **string** → **bool**

```
let search ?(nocase = false) ss s =
  if nocase then
    search' 0 (String.uppercase ss) (String.uppercase s)
  else
    search' 0 ss s
```

Both the pattern and string must be upper case, of course.

Chapter 10 (Finding Permutations)

1

The combinations of a list can be generated by calculating the combinations of the tail. Then consider two possibilities – the head is included in this combination, or it is not:

```
combinations : α list → α list list

let rec combinations l =
  match l with
    [] -> [[]]
  | h::t ->
      let cs = combinations t in
        List.map (fun x -> h :: x) cs @ cs
```

Note the base case is the list containing the empty list, not just the empty list.

2

We build this from perms and the combinations function we just wrote:

```
permicombinations : α list → α list list

let permicombinations l =
  List.concat (List.map perms (combinations l))
```

We used the tail-recursive version of perms, of course.

3

This has roughly the same shape as combinations, with two differences: we keep a counter to make sure the computation ends, and we always add something to the list – either true or false.

```
bool_lists : int → bool list list

let rec bool_lists n =
  match n with
    0 -> [[]]
  | _ ->
      let ls = bool_lists (n - 1) in
        (List.map (fun l -> true :: l) ls) @
        (List.map (fun l -> false :: l) ls)
```

4

We repeatedly swap elements from opposite ends of the sub-array, given an array, offset and length:

```
array_rev : α array → int → int → unit

let array_rev a o l =
  for x = 0 to l / 2 - 1 do
    swap a (o + x) (o + l - x - 1)
  done
```

It is important to make sure it works for the empty range, an even-length sub-array and an odd-length sub-array. You could add detection of invalid arguments to this function.

5

The two functions first and last turn out to be even more awkward than their imperative counterparts. The function first, given a list, returns a tuple of three things: the elements before the "first" item, the first item itself, and those afterward. This is done by reversing the input list and looking for the first appropriate item, since this is easier than looking for the last appropriate item in the original input:

```
first_inner : α list → α list → (α list × α × α list)
first : α list → (α list × α × α list)

let rec first_inner before l =
  match l with
    [] -> raise (Invalid_argument "first_inner")
  | [x] -> (List.rev before, x, [])
  | a::b::t ->
      if b < a
        then (List.rev t, b, (a :: before))
        else first_inner (a :: before) (b :: t)

let first l =
  first_inner [] (List.rev l)
```

The last function is still more verbose: we locate the correct item by sorting and finding the smallest item greater than f. Then we can call split_at to return the item before and after the instance of f.

```
split_at_inner : α list → α → α list → α list × α list
split_at : α → α list → α list × α list
last : α → α list → α list × α × α list

let rec split_at_inner before n l =
  match l with
    [] -> (List.rev before, [])
  | h::t ->
      if h = n
        then (List.rev before, t)
        else split_at_inner (h :: before) n t

let split_at n l =
  split_at_inner [] n l

let last f l =
  match List.filter (fun x -> x > f) (List.sort compare l) with
    [] -> raise (Invalid_argument "last")
  | h::t ->
      let before, after = split_at h l in
        (before, h, after)
```

Now, the `next_permutation` function calls `first` and `last`, and stitches everything together:

```
next_permutation : α list → α list

let next_permutation l =
  let before_f, f, after_f = first l in
    let before_c, c, after_c = last f after_f in
      before_f @ [c] @ List.rev (before_c @ [f] @ after_c)
```

Here is the equivalent `non_increasing` function, which is simple:

```
non_increasing : α list → bool

let rec non_increasing l =
  match l with
    [] | [_] -> true
  | a::b::t -> a >= b && non_increasing (b :: t)
```

The final `all_permutations` function is now easy.

Answers to Questions 163

```
all_permutations_inner : α list list → α list → α list list
all_permutations : α list → α list list

let rec all_permutations_inner a l =
  if non_increasing l then List.rev a else
    let next = next_permutation l in
      all_permutations_inner (next :: a) next

let all_permutations l =
  l :: all_permutations_inner [] l
```

Conclusion: converting an imperative algorithm mechanically to a functional style is not always useful.

Chapter 11 (Making Sets)

1

It is not possible to measure directly the memory used by an OCaml data structure (though one could calculate it by reading the section in the OCaml manual about data representation), but we can use the **Gc** module to measure the number of words allocated whilst building the structure, by using the data in Gc.counters before and after building each structure, and the given formula "memory used since start of program = minor words + major words - promoted words":

Set representation	Memory used (words)
List	150006
Tree	3911613
Red-Black tree	8193038
Hash table	265559

Notice that a huge amount more is required for the tree structures, because every time a new element is inserted, part of the tree is rewritten. In the case of the Red-Black tree, rotations involve allocating new memory too.

2

We can add the type for the union function to our signature:

```
module type SetType2 =
  sig
    type 'a t
    val set_of_list : 'a list -> 'a t
    val list_of_set : 'a t -> 'a list
    val insert : 'a -> 'a t -> 'a t
    val size : 'a t -> int
    val member : 'a -> 'a t -> bool
    val union : 'a t -> 'a t -> 'a t
  end
```

For lists, the union function is easy, we just insert each element of b into the list a. Duplicates will be removed correctly:

```
let union a b = List.fold_left (fun x y -> insert y x) a b
```

For trees and Red-Black trees, we must turn b into a list first, so fold_left can be used, but the solution is broadly the same.

```
let union a b = List.fold_left (fun x y -> insert y x) a (list_of_set b)
```

For hash tables, to preserve the previous tables, we must build lists from both sets, and then build a new set from the concatenation of those too lists:

```
let union a b = set_of_list (list_of_set a @ list_of_set b)
```

The built-in **Set** module, which is considered in Question 3, provides a particularly efficient union operation.

3

We write a version of our set signature which is specialized to integers. Then, we use the syntax given in the question to build the module S. This contains the type S.t, the value S.empty and the functions S.elements, S.add, S.mem, and S.cardinal, which we can use to write the functions to match our signature.

Answers to Questions

```
module IntSet :
  sig
    type t
    val set_of_list : int list -> t
    val list_of_set : t -> int list
    val insert : int -> t -> t
    val size : t -> int
    val member : int -> t -> bool
  end
=
  struct
    module S =
        Set.Make (struct type t = int let compare = compare end)

    type t = S.t

    let list_of_set s = S.elements s

    let set_of_list l = List.fold_right S.add l S.empty

    let member = S.mem

    let insert = S.add

    let size = S.cardinal
  end
```

Now the benchmarking for insertion and membership is simple:

```
benchmark_intset : string → int list → unit

let benchmark_intset name ns =
  let a = Unix.gettimeofday () in
    let set = IntSet.set_of_list ns in
      let b = Unix.gettimeofday () in
        List.iter (fun x -> ignore (IntSet.member x set)) ns;
        let c = Unix.gettimeofday () in
          Printf.printf
            "For %s, insertion took %f, membership %f\n"
            name (b -. a) (c -. b)

let _ =
  benchmark_intset "ordered" nums;
  benchmark_intset "unordered" rand
```

Here is the output:

```
For ordered, insertion took 0.056586, membership 0.019593
For unordered, insertion took 0.087148, membership 0.021295
```

4

We can change the type thus, with BrR for red and BrB for black:

```
type 'a t =
  Lf
| BrR of 'a t * 'a * 'a t
| BrB of 'a t * 'a * 'a t
```

Now, the solutions are tedious to write out, but not difficult. The result is Figure A.2.

Chapter 12 (Playing Games)

1

We already know that O wins 131184 times. By a similar use of num_wins we find that X wins 77904 times. So, as expected, going first is an advantage. We must write another function to find how many draws there are. A board is drawn if it is full but does not contain a winning configuration of either X or O:

```
drawn : tree → int

let rec drawn (Move (b, bs)) =
    (if
        empty b = [] &&
        not (won (List.map (( = ) O) b)) &&
        not (won (List.map (( = ) X) b))
      then 1 else 0)
    +
    List.fold_left ( + ) 0 (List.map drawn bs)
```

This tells us that there are 46080 drawn games. Since each game must be either won or drawn, the total number of possible games is $131184 + 77904 + 46080 = 255168$. We can check this by writing a function to find the terminal nodes directly:

```
terminals : tree → int

let rec terminals (Move (b, bs)) =
  (if bs = [] then 1 else 0) +
  List.fold_left ( + ) 0 (List.map terminals bs)
```

This gives 255168 too.

```ocaml
module SetRedBlack : sig include SetType end =
  struct
    type 'a t =
      Lf
    | BrR of 'a t * 'a * 'a t
    | BrB of 'a t * 'a * 'a t

    let rec list_of_set s =
      match s with
        Lf -> []
      | BrR (l, x, r) | BrB (l, x, r) ->
          x :: list_of_set l @ list_of_set r

    let balance t =
      match t with
        BrB (BrR (BrR (a, x, b), y, c), z, d)
      | BrB (BrR (a, x, BrR (b, y, c)), z, d)
      | BrB (a, x, BrR (BrR (b, y, c), z, d))
      | BrB (a, x, BrR (b, y, BrR (c, z, d))) ->
          BrR (BrB (a, x, b), y, BrB (c, z, d))
      | BrR (a, b, c) -> BrR (a, b, c)
      | BrB (a, b, c) -> BrB (a, b, c)
      | Lf -> Lf

    let rec insert_inner x s =
      match s with
        Lf -> BrR (Lf, x, Lf)
      | BrR (l, y, r) ->
          if x < y
            then balance (BrR (insert_inner x l, y, r))
            else if x > y then balance (BrR (l, y, insert_inner x r))
            else BrR (l, y, r)
      | BrB (l, y, r) ->
          if x < y
            then balance (BrB (insert_inner x l, y, r))
            else if x > y then balance (BrB (l, y, insert_inner x r))
            else BrB (l, y, r)

    let insert x s =
      match insert_inner x s with
        BrR (l, y, r) | BrB (l, y, r) -> BrB (l, y, r)
      | Lf -> assert false

    let rec set_of_list l =
      match l with
        [] -> Lf
      | h::t -> insert h (set_of_list t)

    let rec size s =
      match s with
        Lf -> 0
      | BrR (l, _, r) | BrB (l, _, r) -> 1 + size l + size r

    let rec member x s =
      match s with
        Lf -> false
      | BrR (l, y, r) | BrB (l, y, r) ->
          x = y || if x > y then member x r else member x l
  end
```

Figure A.2

2

We need make only two small changes. Delaying evaluation in the type...

type tree = Move **of** turn list * (unit -> tree list)

...and altering next_moves to insert that delay:

```
next_moves : turn → turn list → tree

let rec next_moves turn board =
  let next =
    fun () ->
      if
        won (List.map (( = ) O) board) ||
        won (List.map (( = ) X) board)
      then
        []
      else
        List.map
          (next_moves (flip_turn turn))
          (List.map (replace turn board) (empty board))
  in
    Move (board, next)
```

Now, we can carefully write a function select_case which, given a starting board such as [E; E; E; E; O; E; E; E; E] and the game tree, returns the portion of the game tree matching that board. Due to laziness, the rest of the tree is now not explored.

We can now alter num_wins easily for the delayed case, and write a function pos_wins which returns the number of wins starting from a position like [E; E; E; E; O; E; E; E; E].

```
select_case : turn list → tree → tree
num_wins : turn → tree → int
pos_wins : turn → turn list → int

let select_case board (Move (_, f)) =
  match List.filter (fun (Move (b, _)) -> b = board) (f ()) with
    [Move (b, g)] -> g ()
  | _ -> raise (Failure "select_case")

let rec num_wins turn (Move (b, bs)) =
  (if won (List.map (( = ) turn) b) then 1 else 0) +
  List.fold_left ( + ) 0 (List.map (num_wins turn) (bs ()))

let pos_wins turn pos =
  List.fold_left ( + ) 0
    (List.map (num_wins turn) (select_case pos game_tree))
```

Similarly, we can modify the drawn function to work with the new lazy structure, and write a new function draws to count the drawn positions from a given starting board such as [E; E; E; E; O; E; E; E; E]:

```
drawn : tree → int
draws : turn list → int

let rec drawn (Move (b, bs)) =
    (if
        empty b = [] &&
        not (won (List.map (( = ) O) b)) &&
        not (won (List.map (( = ) X) b))
     then 1 else 0)
  +
    List.fold_left ( + ) 0 (List.map drawn (bs ()))

let draws pos =
  List.fold_left ( + ) 0
    (List.map drawn (select_case pos game_tree))
```

Now we can define starting boards for the centre spot, the middle of a side, and a corner. We can now use pos_wins and draws, taking account of symmetry to enumerate all the cases:

```
let centre = [E; E; E; E; O; E; E; E; E]

let side = [E; O; E; E; E; E; E; E; E]

let corner = [O; E; E; E; E; E; E; E; E]

let centre_x_wins = pos_wins X centre

let centre_o_wins = pos_wins O centre

let centre_drawn = draws centre

let side_x_wins = pos_wins X side * 4

let side_o_wins = pos_wins O side * 4

let side_drawn = draws side * 4

let corner_x_wins = pos_wins X corner * 4

let corner_o_wins = pos_wins O corner * 4

let corner_drawn = draws side * 4
```

This gives the following:

```
val centre_x_wins : int = 5616
val centre_o_wins : int = 15648
val centre_drawn : int = 4608
val side_x_wins : int = 40704
val side_o_wins : int = 56928
val side_drawn : int = 20736
val corner_x_wins : int = 31584
val corner_o_wins : int = 58608
val corner_drawn : int = 20736
```

The total is 255168, of course.

3

The strategy of using the magic square representation is to build a problem which is *isomorphic* (has the same essential characteristics – literally *the same shape*) to the original one, but is easier to work with. Before building the tree tree, we will need five little functions:

- sum, which checks if a list sums to 15;
- threes, which finds all the combinations of numbers from a list of numbers which are of length three (the combinations function is from Chapter 10);
- won, which uses threes to check if a list of integers contains a combination of three numbers which sum to 15;
- drawn which, given the integer lists for X and O, works out if the game has been drawn; and
- possibles which, given all the non-empty squares, lists the empty ones.

```
sum : int list → bool
threes : α list → α list list
won : int list → bool
drawn : α list → β list → bool
possibles : int list → int list

let sum l = List.fold_left ( + ) 0 l = 15

let threes l = List.filter (fun l -> length l = 3) (combinations l)

let won l = List.mem true (List.map sum (threes l))

let drawn l l' = length l + length l' = 9

let possibles all =
  List.filter
    (fun x -> not (List.mem x all))
    [1; 2; 3; 4; 5; 6; 7; 8; 9]
```

Now, the type contains a list of X positions, a list of O positions, and the list of child nodes:

```
type tree = Move of int list * int list * tree list
```

We do not need a type for the turn this time – we can just use a boolean. The function next_moves follows the usual pattern – if the game is won or drawn, the list of child nodes is empty. Otherwise, we build child nodes for each possible position the next player could place his piece.

```
next_moves : int list → int list → bool → tree
game_tree : tree

let rec next_moves xs os o_is_playing =
  let next =
    if won xs || won os || drawn xs os then [] else
      if o_is_playing
        then
          List.map
            (fun new_os -> next_moves xs new_os (not o_is_playing))
            (List.map (fun q -> q :: os) (possibles (xs @ os)))
        else
          List.map
            (fun new_xs -> next_moves new_xs os (not o_is_playing))
            (List.map (fun q -> q :: xs) (possibles (xs @ os)))
  in
    Move (xs, os, next)

let game_tree = next_moves [] [] true
```

The game tree is shown in Figure A.3. We can write a simple xwins function to test our new function returns the same result as the original.

```
xwins : tree → int

let rec xwins (Move (xs, os, cs)) =
  (if won xs then 1 else 0) +
  List.fold_left ( + ) 0 (List.map xwins cs)
```

Chapter 13 (Representing Documents)

1

Writing T for the trailer dictionary, we have the graph T $\to$ 2 $\to$ 3 $\longleftrightarrow$ 1 $\to$ 4.

2

These can be written out by reference to the data structure:

```
val game_tree : tree =
  Move ([], [],
   [Move ([], [1],
     [Move ([2], [1],
      [Move ([2], [3; 1],
       [Move ([4; 2], [3; 1],
        [Move ([4; 2], [5; 3; 1],
         [Move ([6; 4; 2], [5; 3; 1],
          [Move ([6; 4; 2], [7; 5; 3; 1], []);
           Move ([6; 4; 2], [8; 5; 3; 1],
            [Move ([7; 6; 4; 2], [8; 5; 3; 1], []);
             Move ([9; 6; 4; 2], [8; 5; 3; 1], [])]);
           Move ([6; 4; 2], [9; 5; 3; 1], [])]);
          Move ([7; 4; 2], [5; 3; 1],
           [Move ([7; 4; 2], [6; 5; 3; 1],
            [Move ([8; 7; 4; 2], [6; 5; 3; 1],
             [Move ([8; 7; 4; 2], [9; 6; 5; 3; 1], [])]);
             Move ([9; 7; 4; 2], [6; 5; 3; 1], [])]);
            Move ([7; 4; 2], [8; 5; 3; 1],
             [Move ([6; 7; 4; 2], [8; 5; 3; 1], []);
              Move ([9; 7; 4; 2], [8; 5; 3; 1], [])]);
            Move ([7; 4; 2], [9; 5; 3; 1], [])]);
          Move ([8; 4; 2], [5; 3; 1],
           [Move ([8; 4; 2], [6; 5; 3; 1],
            [Move ([7; 8; 4; 2], [6; 5; 3; 1],
             [Move ([7; 8; 4; 2], [9; 6; 5; 3; 1], [])]);
             Move ([9; 8; 4; 2], [6; 5; 3; 1], [])]);
            Move ([8; 4; 2], [7; 5; 3; 1], []);
            Move ([8; 4; 2], [9; 5; 3; 1], [])]);
          Move ([9; 4; 2], [5; 3; 1], [])]);
         ...]);
        ...]);
       ...]);
      ...]);
     ...])
```

Figure A.3

- Name "/Name"
- String "Quartz Crystal"
- Dictionary [("/Type", Name "/ObjStm"); ("/N", Integer 100); ("/First", Integer 807); ("/Last", Integer 1836); ("/Filter", Name "/FlateDecode")]
- Array [Integer 1; Integer 2; Float 1.5; String "black"]
- Array [Integer 1; Indirect 2]

In the last two examples, we assumed integer where appropriate. Notice that in the last example, the parsing is somewhat ambiguous – we would need to read all the way to the R to be sure it was not an array of several integers.

3

Consider the tree Br (Br (Lf, 1, Lf), 2, Br (Lf, 3, Lf)). We will represent it by using nested PDF dictionaries. A branch will have a /Type key with value /Br. It will have /Left and /Right entries for the sub-trees. A leaf is indicated simply by /Lf. In the PDF file we would write it like this:

```
<</Type /Br
  /Value 2
  /Left <</Type /Br /Value 1 /Left /Lf /Right /Lf>>
  /Right <</Type /Br /Value 3 /Left /Lf /Right /Lf>>>>
```

To construct it from our data type in OCaml:

```
let tree =
  Pdf.Dictionary
    [("/Type", Pdf.Name "/Br");
     ("/Value", Pdf.Integer 2);
     ("/Left",
        Pdf.Dictionary
          [("/Type", Pdf.Name "/Br");
           ("/Value", Pdf.Integer 1);
           ("/Left", Pdf.Name "/Lf");
           ("/Right", Pdf.Name "/Lf")]);
     ("/Right",
        Pdf.Dictionary
          [("/Type", Pdf.Name "/Br");
           ("/Value", Pdf.Integer 3);
           ("/Left", Pdf.Name "/Lf");
           ("/Right", Pdf.Name "/Lf")])]
```

4

We must search for dictionary entries inside Pdf.Dictionary, of course, but also inside Pdf.Stream, which contains a dictionary, and Pdf.Array which may do so too. Two mutually-recursive functions will do:

```
rotate_90 : Pdf.pdfobject → Pdf.pdfobject
rotate_90_dict : string × Pdf.pdfobject → string × Pdf.pdfobject

let rec rotate_90 obj =
  match obj with
    Pdf.Array objs ->
      Pdf.Array (List.map rotate_90 objs)
  | Pdf.Dictionary objs ->
      Pdf.Dictionary (List.map rotate_90_dict objs)
  | Pdf.Stream (dict, str) ->
      Pdf.Stream (rotate_90 dict, str)
  | x -> x

and rotate_90_dict (k, v) =
  match k with
    "/Rotate" -> ("/Rotate", Pdf.Integer 90)
  | _ -> (k, rotate_90 v)
```

Chapter 14 (Writing Documents)

1

We can alter the functions `string_of_array` and `string_of_dictionary` to simply not output the space preceding the closing bracket. To remove the initial space requires a little trick. We inspect the length of the buffer to determine if we are about to output the first item. In that case, no space is written. This is shown in Figure A.4.

2

The full code can be found in the online resources. We make the following changes:

- Change `/Count` from 1 to 3.
- Move the `/Resources` to its own object, number 5.
- Write two new pages, objects 6 and 7.
- Write two new page content streams, 8 and 9.
- Change the `/Size` from 5 to 10 to account for the new objects.

3

The full code can be found in the online resources. See the hint for a little more help.

Chapter 15 (Pretty Pictures)

1

Since we are working with circles, let us define π:

```
string_of_array : Pdf.pdfobject list → string
string_of_dictionary : (string ×Pdf.pdfobject) list → string

let rec string_of_array a =
  let b = Buffer.create 100 in
    Buffer.add_string b "[";
    List.iter
      (fun s ->
        if Buffer.length b > 1 then Buffer.add_char b ' ';
        Buffer.add_string b (string_of_pdfobject s))
      a;
    Buffer.add_string b "]";
    Buffer.contents b

and string_of_dictionary d =
  let b = Buffer.create 100 in
    Buffer.add_string b "<<";
    List.iter
      (fun (k, v) ->
        if Buffer.length b > 2 then Buffer.add_char b ' ';
        Buffer.add_string b k;
        Buffer.add_char b ' ';
        Buffer.add_string b (string_of_pdfobject v))
      d;
    Buffer.add_string b ">>";
    Buffer.contents b
```

Figure A.4

```
pi : float

let pi = 4. *. atan 1.
```

We can write a simple function to return the point at a given angle, distance r from point (x, y):

```
point : float → float → float → float → float × float

let point x y r angle =
  (cos angle *. r +. x, sin angle *. r +. y)
```

Now, we can build a list of all these points, remembering to stop before we have been around the whole circle. The argument step is the angle between successive points.

```
points : float → float → float → float → (float × float) list

let points x y r step =
  let n = ref 0
  and points = ref [] in
    while float_of_int !n *. step < 2. *. r *. pi do
      points := point x y r (float_of_int !n *. step) :: !points;
      n := !n + 1
    done;
    !points
```

Finally, we generate a Move to the first points, Lines to the rest, and a final Close.

```
circle : float → float → float → Pdfpage.t list
circle_filled : Pdfpage.t list

let circle x y r =
  match points x y r (pi /. 20.) with
    (x, y)::lines ->
      Pdfpage.Move (x, y) ::
      List.map (fun (x, y) -> Pdfpage.Line (x, y)) lines @
      [Pdfpage.Close]
  | _ ->
      assert false        the points function should never return an empty list

let circle_filled =
  circle 300. 300. 100. @ [Pdfpage.Fill]
```

For our example, we made a filled circle of radius 100 centred at (300, 300) with Pdfpage.Fill:

2

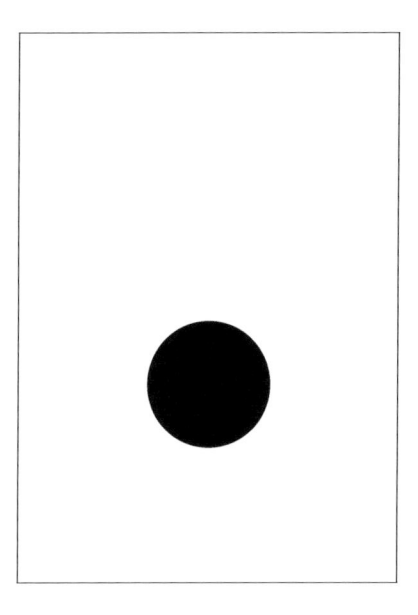

First, a function to build a pseudo-random circle somewhere on our page, making sure to overlap the edges:

```
random_circle : unit → Pdfpage.t list

let random_circle () =
  let x = Random.float 700. -. 50.
  and y = Random.float 1000. -. 50.
  and r = Random.float 100. +. 20. in
    circle x y r
```

Now, a little utility function to build a list of n things when given a function which generates them, such as random_circle:

```
many : (unit → α) → int → α list

let rec many f n =
  match n with
    0 -> []
  | _ -> f () :: many f (n - 1)
```

Now it is simple to build a hundred random grey filled circles and append them all together with List.concat:

```
many_circles : Pdfpage.t list

let many_circles =
  List.concat
    (List.map
       (fun l ->
         List.append
           (Pdfpage.FillColour (Random.float 1.) :: l)
           [Pdfpage.Fill])
       (many random_circle 100))
```

3

We can add FillColourRGB **of** float * float * float and StrokeColourRGB **of** float * float * float to the data type and associated functions, and then modify our previous example:

```
many_circles_colour : Pdfpage.t list

let many_circles_colour =
  List.concat
    (List.map
      (fun l ->
        List.append
          (Pdfpage.FillColourRGB
            (Random.float 1., Random.float 1., Random.float 1.)
            :: l)
          [Pdfpage.Fill])
      (many random_circle 100))
```

If you are reading the PDF ebook version of this book, the following image is in colour:

4

We add `LineWidth` **of** `float` to the data type and associated functions. Now we set the line width and stroke colour and draw the large circle:

```
big_circle : Pdfpage.t
circle_over_circles : Pdfpage.t

let big_circle =
    [Pdfpage.LineWidth 5.; Pdfpage.StrokeColour 0.]
  @ circle 300. 400. 150.
  @ [Pdfpage.Stroke]

let circle_over_circles =
  many_circles_colour @ big_circle
```

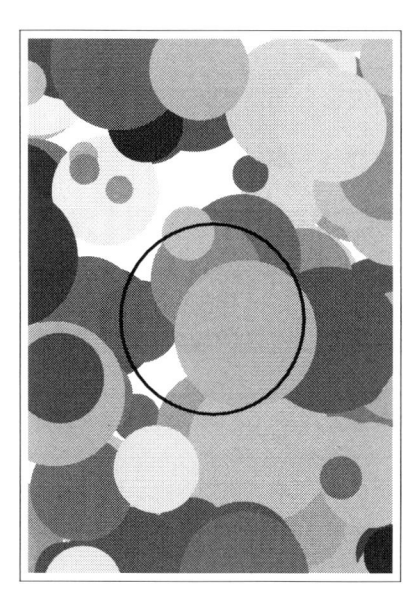

5

We add `SetClip` to the data type and associated functions. Then we set the clip before stroking.

```
big_clipping_circle : Pdfpage.t list
clipped : Pdfpage.t list

let big_clipping_circle =
  [Pdfpage.LineWidth 1.; Pdfpage.StrokeColour 0.] @
  circle 300. 400. 150. @
  [Pdfpage.SetClip; Pdfpage.Stroke]

let clipped =
  big_clipping_circle @ many_circles_colour
```

The single path is used both for clipping and for the stroke:

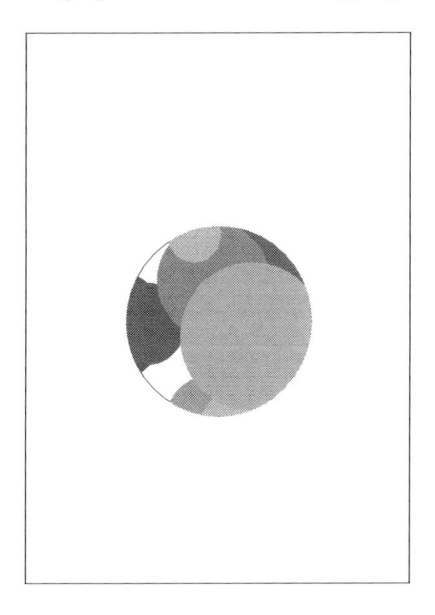

Chapter 16 (Adding Text)

1

We can pull out font size, line spacing and margin easily, defining them at the top of the page. The text width is derived from the page width and margin. The maximum number of characters in a line can be calculated using the formula given in the question:

```
let font_size = 10.0

let line_spacing = 1.1

let margin = 40.0

let text_width = page_width -. margin -. margin

let max_chars = int_of_float (text_width /. font_size *. (5. /. 3))
```

We can now insert these new names into typeset_line_at:

```
Pdfpage.SetTextPosition (margin, y);
Pdfpage.SetFontAndSize ("/F0", font_size);
```

We pass max_chars to clean_lines and alter our call to downfrom:

```
let ls = clean_lines (lines max_chars words) in
```

```
         downfrom
           (font_size *. line_spacing)
           (page_height -. margin -. line_spacing) (List.length ls) 0
```

Here is an example of the new program, with text typeset on a much smaller page (it runs off the bottom, of course):

2

We can implement this by manually inserting space characters into the buffer in lines_inner following every newline (i.e. at the beginning of the second and subsequent paragraphs). This is shown in Figure A.5. Notice the use of an optional argument in lines. We can now alter one line in typeset_page:

```
    let ls = clean_lines (lines max_chars ~indent:8 words) in
```

The result is shown in Figure A.6.

3

The page height can be calculated easily:

```
    let text_height = page_height -. margin -. margin
```

Now, we can use Pdfpage.SetCharacterSpacing in typeset_line_at, adding an extra argument for the spacing:

```
lines_inner : Pdfpage.t list
lines : float → ?indent:int → string list → string list list

let rec lines_inner ls b width indent words =
  match words with
    [] ->
      if Buffer.length b > 0 then
        List.rev (Partial (Buffer.contents b) :: ls)
      else
        List.rev ls
  | "\n"::t ->
      let b' = Buffer.create width in
        for x = 1 to indent do Buffer.add_char b' ' ' done;
        lines_inner
          (Partial (Buffer.contents b) :: ls) b' width indent t
  | word::t ->
      if Buffer.length b = 0 && String.length word > width then
        lines_inner
          (Full word :: ls) (Buffer.create width) width indent t
      else if String.length word + Buffer.length b < width then
        begin
          Buffer.add_string b word;
          if Buffer.length b < width then Buffer.add_char b ' ';
          lines_inner ls b width indent t
        end
      else
        lines_inner
          (Full (Buffer.contents b) :: ls)
          (Buffer.create width) width indent (word :: t)

let lines width ?(indent=0) words =
  lines_inner [] (Buffer.create width) width indent words
```

Figure A.5

One morning, when Gregor Samsa woke from troubled dreams, he found himself
transformed in his bed into a horrible vermin. He lay on his armour-like back, and
if he lifted his head a little he could see his brown belly, slightly domed and
divided by arches into stiff sections. The bedding was hardly able to cover it and
seemed ready to slide off any moment. His many legs, pitifully thin compared with
the size of the rest of him, waved about helplessly as he looked.

"What's happened to me?" he thought. It wasn't a dream. His room, a proper
human room although a little too small, lay peacefully between its four familiar
walls. A collection of textile samples lay spread out on the table - Samsa was a
travelling salesman - and above it there hung a picture that he had recently cut
out of an illustrated magazine and housed in a nice, gilded frame. It showed a
lady fitted out with a fur hat and fur boa who sat upright, raising a heavy fur
muff that covered the whole of her lower arm towards the viewer.

Gregor then turned to look out the window at the dull weather. Drops of
rain could be heard hitting the pane, which made him feel quite sad. "How about if
I sleep a little bit longer and forget all this nonsense", he thought, but that
was something he was unable to do because he was used to sleeping on his right,
and in his present state couldn't get into that position. However hard he threw
himself onto his right, he always rolled back to where he was. He must have tried
it a hundred times, shut his eyes so that he wouldn't have to look at the
floundering legs, and only stopped when he began to feel a mild, dull pain there
that he had never felt before.

"Oh, God", he thought, "what a strenuous career it is that I've chosen!
Travelling day in and day out. Doing business like this takes much more effort
than doing your own business at home, and on top of that there's the curse of
travelling, worries about making train connections, bad and irregular food,
contact with different people all the time so that you can never get to know
anyone or become friendly with them. It can all go to Hell!" He felt a slight itch
up on his belly; pushed himself slowly up on his back towards the headboard so
that he could lift his head better; found where the itch was, and saw that it was
covered with lots of little white spots which he didn't know what to make of; and
when he tried to feel the place with one of his legs he drew it quickly back
because as soon as he touched it he was overcome by a cold shudder.

He slid back into his former position. "Getting up early all the time", he
thought, "it makes you stupid. You've got to get enough sleep. Other travelling
salesmen live a life of luxury. For instance, whenever I go back to the guest
house during the morning to copy out the contract, these gentlemen are always
still sitting there eating their breakfasts. I ought to just try that with my
boss; I'd get kicked out on the spot. But who knows, maybe that would be the best
thing for me. If I didn't have my parents to think about I'd have given in my
notice a long time ago, I'd have gone up to the boss and told him just what I
think, tell him everything I would, let him know just what I feel. He'd fall right
off his desk! And it's a funny sort of business to be sitting up there at your
desk, talking down at your subordinates from up there, especially when you have to
go right up close because the boss is hard of hearing. Well, there's still some
hope; once I've got the money together to pay off my parents' debt to him -
another five or six years I suppose - that's definitely what I'll do. That's when
I'll make the big change. First of all though, I've got to get up, my train leaves
at five."

Figure A.6

```
typeset_line_at : float → string → float → Pdfpage.t list

let typeset_line_at spacing line y =
  [Pdfpage.BeginText;
   Pdfpage.SetCharacterSpacing spacing;
   Pdfpage.SetTextPosition (margin, y);
   Pdfpage.SetFontAndSize ("/F0", font_size);
   Pdfpage.ShowText line;
   Pdfpage.EndText]
```

The spacing is calculated as prescribed, only for `Full` lines:

```
calculate_spacing : float → string → float

let calculate_spacing width line =
  match line with
    Full s ->
      float (width - String.length s) /.
      float (String.length s - 1) *. font_size *. (3. /. 5.)
  | Partial s -> 0.
```

In a revised `typeset_page`, we can calculate the correct spacings, passing them to `typeset_line_at`:

```
typeset_page : string → Pdfpage.t list

let typeset_page text =
  let words = words_of_input (Input.input_of_string text) in
  let ls = lines max_chars ~indent:8 words in
  let spacings = List.map (calculate_spacing max_chars) ls in
  let positions =
    downfrom
      (font_size *. line_spacing)
      (page_height -. margin -. line_spacing) (List.length ls) 0
  in
    List.concat
      (List.map3
         typeset_line_at spacings (clean_lines ls) positions)
```

Here is an example page. You can see that the lines are fully justified – flush to the left and right margins.

> One morning, when Gregor Samsa woke from troubled dreams, he found himself transformed in his bed into a horrible vermin. He lay on his armour-like back, and if he lifted his head a little he could see his brown belly, slightly domed and divided by arches into stiff sections. The bedding was hardly able to cover it and seemed ready to slide off any moment. His many legs, pitifully thin compared with the size of the rest of him, waved about helplessly as he looked.
>
> "What's happened to me?" he thought. It wasn't a dream. His room, a proper human room although a little too small, lay peacefully between its four familiar walls. A collection of textile samples lay spread out on the table - Samsa was a travelling salesman - and above it there hung a picture that he had recently cut out of an illustrated magazine and housed in a nice, gilded frame. It showed a lady fitted out with a fur hat and fur boa who sat upright, raising a heavy fur muff that covered the whole of her lower arm towards the viewer.
>
> Gregor then turned to look out the window at the dull weather. Drops of rain could be heard hitting the pane, which made him feel quite sad. "How about if I sleep a little bit longer and forget all this nonsense", he thought, but that was something he was unable to do because he was used to sleeping on his right, and in his present state couldn't get into that position. However hard he threw himself onto his right, he always rolled back to where he was. He must have tried it a hundred times, shut his eyes so that he wouldn't have to look at the floundering legs, and only stopped when he began to feel a mild, dull pain there that he had never felt before.
>
> "Oh, God", he thought, "what a strenuous career it is that I've chosen! Travelling day in and day out. Doing business like this takes much more effort than doing your own business at home, and on top of that there's the curse of travelling, worries about making train connections, bad and irregular food, contact with different people all the time so that you can never get to know anyone or become friendly with them. It can all go to Hell!" He felt a slight itch up on his belly; pushed himself slowly up on his back towards the headboard so that he could lift his head better; found where the itch was, and saw that it was covered with lots of little white spots which he didn't know what to make of; and when he tried to feel the place with one of his legs he drew it quickly back because as soon as he touched it he was overcome by a cold shudder.
>
> He slid back into his former position. "Getting up early all the time", he thought, "it makes you stupid. You've got to get enough sleep. Other travelling salesmen live a life of luxury. For instance, whenever I go back to the guest house during the morning to copy out the contract, these gentlemen are always still sitting there eating their breakfasts. I ought to just try that with my boss; I'd get kicked out on the spot. But who knows, maybe that would be the best thing for me. If I didn't have my parents to think about I'd have given in my notice a long time ago, I'd have gone up to the boss and told him just what I think, tell him everything I would, let him know just what I feel. He'd fall right off his desk! And it's a funny sort of business to be sitting up there at your desk, talking down at your subordinates from up there, especially when you have to go right up close because the boss is hard of hearing. Well, there's still some hope; once I've got the money together to pay off my parents' debt to him - another five or six years I suppose - that's definitely what I'll do. That's when I'll make the big change. First of all though, I've got to get up, my train leaves at five."

4

The answer to this question is too long to be contained in the text. Consult the online resources for the program itself. An example multi-page output is shown in Figure A.7.

One morning, when Gregor Samsa woke from troubled dreams, he found himself transformed in his bed into a horrible vermin. He lay on his armour-like back, and if he lifted his head a little he could see his brown belly, slightly domed and divided by arches into stiff sections. The bedding was hardly able to cover it and seemed ready to slide off any moment. His many legs, pitifully thin compared with the size of the rest of him, waved about helplessly as he looked.

"What's happened to me?" he thought. It wasn't a dream. His room, a proper human room although a little too small, lay peacefully between its four familiar walls. A collection of textile samples lay spread out on the table - Samsa was a travelling salesman - and above it there hung a picture that he had recently cut out of an illustrated magazine and housed in a nice, gilded frame. It showed a lady fitted out with a fur hat and fur boa who sat upright, raising a heavy fur muff that covered the whole of her lower arm towards the viewer.

Gregor then turned to look out the window at the dull weather. Drops of rain could be heard hitting the pane, which made him feel quite sad. "How about if I sleep a little bit longer and forget all this nonsense", he thought, but that was something he was unable to do because he was used to sleeping on his right, and in his present state couldn't get into that position. However hard he threw himself onto his right, he always rolled back to where he was. He must have tried it a hundred times, shut his eyes so that he wouldn't have to look at the floundering legs, and only stopped when he began to feel a mild, dull pain there that he had never felt before.

"Oh, God", he thought, "what a strenuous career it is that I've chosen! Travelling day in and day out. Doing business like this takes much more effort than doing your own business at home, and on top of that there's the curse of travelling, worries about making train connections, bad and irregular food, contact with different people all the time so that you can never get to know anyone or become friendly with them. It can all go to Hell!" He felt a slight itch up on his belly; pushed himself slowly up on his back towards the headboard so that he could lift his head better; found where the itch was, and saw that it was covered with lots of little white spots which he didn't know what to make of; and when he tried to feel the place with one of his legs he drew it quickly back because as soon as he touched it he was overcome by a cold shudder.

He slid back into his former position. "Getting up early all the time", he thought, "it makes you stupid. You've got to get enough sleep. Other travelling salesmen live a life of luxury. For instance, whenever I go back to the guest house during the morning to copy out the contract, these gentlemen are always still sitting there eating their breakfasts. I ought to just try that with my boss; I'd get kicked out on the spot. But who knows, maybe that would be the best thing for me. If I didn't have my parents to think about I'd have given in my notice a long time ago, I'd have gone up to the boss and told him just what I think, tell him everything I would, let him know just what I feel. He'd fall right off his desk! And it's a funny sort of business to be sitting up there at your desk, talking down at your subordinates from up there, especially when you have to go right up close because the boss is hard of hearing. Well, there's still some hope; once I've got the money together to pay off my parents' debt to him - another five or six years I suppose - that's definitely what I'll do. That's when I'll make the big change. First of all though, I've got to get up, my train leaves at five."

Figure A.7

Hints for Questions

Chapter 1
Unravelling "Fold"

1

What must the accumulator start at? What operation must we perform each time? Consider the `sum` function from the text as a starting point.

2

We need to ignore each element, just incrementing an accumulator when we see each one. The final value of the accumulator will then be the length of the list. What is the initial accumulator?

3

A good way to deal with the fact that an empty list has no last element would be to return an **option** type.

4

These sorts of folds producing lists have an accumulator which is a list type – you might start at the empty list.

5

The type will be the same as for `List.mem`. How do we keep track of whether or not we have seen a matching element? What is the initial accumulator?

6

This will involve a string accumulator and the string concatenation operator. How to we ensure there is not an excess space before or after the sentence?

7

The built-in `max` operator returns the larger of two values.

8

You can use the Standard Library function `Unix.gettimeofday` to help time the functions.

Chapter 2
Being Lazy

1

This is very similar to `lseq` in the text.

2

Construct by analogy to the same function on ordinary lists. Remember one needs to force evaluation to get at the tail.

3

How do we know when we have reached the end of the input list and must start again? What do we do if the input list is empty?

4

Consider the definition of fibonacci numbers. Split into a function which builds the lazy list given two numbers, and the construction of the list itself.

5

The type of the function will be α lazylist $\to \alpha$ lazylist $\times\ \alpha$ lazylist. You will need to force the evaluation of the tail of the input list twice to yield the heads of the two output lists, and then work out how to produce the tails.

6

Write a function which builds the alphabetic string from a number. Then, some of the generic lazy list handling functions from the text can be used to build the lazy list itself.

Chapter 3
Named Tuples with Records

1

What is a reference really?

2

Look at the functions `Unix.time` and `Unix.localtime`. You will need to deal with conversion of day-of-week and month from integers to strings yourself, but this is not difficult.

4

Records types can be parametrized, just like other data types.

5

See the documentation for a) `Gc.stat` and b) `Gc.set` and `Gc.get`.

Chapter 4
Generalized Input/Output

1

A simple modification of `input_of_string`.

2

Use a **Buffer.t** to accumulate the characters.

3

The new field will have type **unit** $\to$ **char option**.

4

The new field will have type **unit** $\to$ **int**. For `input_of_channel` and `input_of_string`, use exception handling to return the special value. Consider giving the special value -1 a name.

5

Check for a newline character on each `input_char`, raising `End_of_file`. Can you use `input_string` with the new channel you have created to return the user input?

6

The **Buffer** module already contains ideal functions for this.

Chapter 5
Streams of Bits

1

What is the test for being able to read a whole byte at a time? What do we do if the condition is met? If it is not?

2

Just replace the integer functions with ones from the **Int32** module.

Hints for Questions

3

What is the test for being able to write a whole byte at a time? What do we do if the condition is met? If it is not?

4

Just replace the integer functions with ones from the **Int32** module.

5

Try adding a `rewind` method to your `output` type, which goes back one byte. Now extend `output_-of_bytes` appropriately.

Chapter 6
Compressing Data

1

Use list processing functions over a list of integers representing the data. For testing purposes, re-use our `int_list_of_string` and `string_of_-int_list` functions.

2

Carefully define a suitable data type for the tree – the data will all be at the fringes of the tree, since no code is a prefix of another. Write a function to add a code to the tree. Now, repeated insertion can be used to build the whole tree.

4

We can re-use the `read_up_to` function, building up two histograms – one for white runs and one for black runs.

Chapter 7
Labelled and Optional Arguments

1

Consider what happens if α is **int**.

2

Perhaps define one or more new types.

3

Consider which functions have two or more arguments of the same type. We can add labels to those arguments only and wrap the function up.

4

We can use an optional argument for the accumulator.

Chapter 8
Formatted Printing

1

Consider `Printf.bprintf` as a way to accumulate the parts. What is special about the last element? What if there is no last element?

2

There is a format specifier for hexadecimal numbers. Consider what happens with very small character codes.

Chapter 9
Searching for Things

1

The `at` function from the chapter may be re-used here, in both parts of the question.

2

Start by writing a function which gives the length of the longest prefix of a pattern at the beginning of a list. Now wrap it in another which works through the whole list.

3

The expression `Unix.gettimeofday ()` gives a floating-point number representing the current time.

4

Add a case to the inner match. It must manually check the next letter in the pattern matches the next letter in the string (if it exists).

5

This does not require altering the search code itself – one can just preprocess the pattern and string. There is a function `String.uppercase` in the Standard Library.

Chapter 10
Finding Permutations

1

What is the base case? For the main case, first calculate the combinations of the tail by recursion. What can you do now?

2

You can build this from functions we have already written.

3

What is the base case? You will need to keep a counter to make sure we only generate lists of the given length.

4

Consider using the `swap` function we defined in the main text.

5

Instead of using indices for the "first" and "last", use the values themselves. Pull the list representing the old permutation apart, and rearrange it until you have the next.

Chapter 11
Making Sets

1

In the documentation for the **Gc** module, you will find the function `Gc.counters` and a description of how to calculate the total amount of memory allocated since the program began.

2

Add a `union` function to the signature, with the type $\alpha\ t \rightarrow \alpha\ t \rightarrow \alpha\ t$ and then a `union` function to the struct for each set representation.

3

You can include the given code inside the structure of the new module. Now, you can set the type t to be equal to S.t, the type of these new sets.

4

Alter the type first. The changes to each function then follow relatively easily.

Chapter 12
Playing Games

1

We already have code to find the number of X wins. What are the conditions for a game being drawn?

2

It is only necessary to alter the type `tree` and the function `next_moves`, and only a little. Now we need a function to extract the part of the tree which begins with O in the centre slot. Once we have this, simple modifications of our functions for counting wins and draws will do the job.

Hints for Questions

3

There is no need to worry about the order of the numbers in the square – the tree will have the same essential characteristics regardless.

Chapter 13
Representing Documents

3

A structure built from nested dictionaries would be suitable.

4

Consider everywhere a dictionary entry might appear. The function or functions will be recursive, following the general pattern of the data structure.

Chapter 14
Writing Documents

1

Removing the space at the end is simple. How can we detect if we are about to output the first item, and thus do not want a space?

2

Remember to alter the /Size entry, and to change /Indirect entries as required to reflect the new structure.

3

For the content stream in the "Hello, World!" file, one long row is sufficient. However, when encoding other example content streams, consult the PDF specification to ensure the file is still valid. To test, open in your favourite PDF reader.

Chapter 15
Pretty Pictures

1

We need to generate a set of points on the circle, and then they can be built into a path with Move, Line, and Close. This path can then be used with Fill to build the final page content.

2

First write a function to generate a path for a pseudo-random circle using a function we have previously written. Now FillColour and Fill can be added for each one, and the final list of operators produced.

3

We add FillColourRGB and StrokeColourRGB items to the data type and its associated functions. Then we can substitute them into the previous answer.

Chapter 16
Adding Text

1

You need to alter typeset_line_at, clean_lines, and downfrom once you have defined the new values.

2

Try just adding eight space characters after each new line in lines_inner.

3

If there are n characters, we must insert $n - 1$ pieces of space between them, each of equal size.

4

To make the construction of the multipage document simpler, consider choosing carefully the order (and hence numbering) of the objects in the file.

Coping with Errors

It is very hard to write even small programs correctly the first time. An unfortunate but inevitable part of programming is the location and fixing of mistakes. OCaml has a range of messages to help you with this process.

Here are descriptions of the common messages OCaml prints when a program cannot be accepted or when running it causes a problem (a so-called "run-time error"). We also describe warnings OCaml prints to alert the programmer to a program which, though it can be accepted for evaluation, might contain mistakes.

ERRORS

These are messages printed when an expression could not be accepted for evaluation, due to being malformed in some way. No evaluation is attempted. You must fix the expression and try again.

Syntax error

This error occurs when OCaml finds that the program text contains things which are not valid words (such as **if**, **let** etc.) or other basic parts of the language, or when they exist in invalid combinations – this is known as *syntax*. Check carefully and try again.

```
        OCaml

#1 +;;
Error: syntax error
```

OCaml has underlined where it thinks the error is. Since this error occurs for a wide range of different mistakes and problems, the underlining may not pinpoint the exact position of your mistake.

Unbound value ...

This error occurs when you have mentioned a name which has not been defined (technically "bound to a value"). This might happen if you have mistyped the name.

```
        OCaml
```

```
# x + 1;;
Error: Unbound value x
```

In our example x is not defined, so it has been underlined.

This expression has type … but an expression was expected of type …

You will see this error very frequently. It occurs when the expression's syntax is correct (i.e. it is made up of valid words and constructs), and OCaml has moved on to type-checking the expression prior to evaluation. If there is a problem with type-checking, OCaml shows you where a mismatch between the expected and actual type occurred.

OCaml

```
# 1 + true;;
Error: This expression has type bool but an expression was expected of type
       int
```

In this example, OCaml is looking for an integer on the right hand side of the + operator, and finds something of type **bool** instead.

It is not always as easy to spot the real source of the problem, especially if the function is recursive. Nevertheless, a careful look at the program will often shine light on the problem – look at each function and its arguments, and try to find your mistake.

This function is applied to too many arguments

Exactly what it says. The function name is underlined.

OCaml

```
# let f x = x + 1;;
val f : int -> int = <fun>
# f x y;;
Error: This function is applied to too many arguments;
maybe you forgot a `;'
```

The phrase "maybe you forgot a ';' " applies to imperative programs where accidently missing out a ';' between successive function applications might commonly lead to this error.

Unbound constructor …

This occurs when a constructor name is used which is not defined.

OCaml

```
# type t = Roof | Wall | Floor;;
```

```
type t = Roof | Wall | Floor
# Window;;
Error: Unbound constructor Window
```

OCaml knows it is a constructor name because it has an initial capital letter.

The constructor ... expects ... argument(s), but is applied here to ... argument(s)

This error occurs when the wrong kind of data is given to a constructor for a type. It is just another type error, but we get a specialized message.

>   OCaml

```
# type p = A of int | B of bool;;
type p = A of int | B of bool
# A;;
Error: The constructor A expects 1 argument(s),
       but is applied here to 0 argument(s)
```

RUN-TIME ERRORS

In any programming language powerful enough to be of use, some errors cannot be detected before attempting evaluation of an expression (until "run-time"). The exception mechanism is for handling and recovering from these kinds of problems.

Stack overflow during evaluation (looping recursion?)

This occurs if the function builds up a working expression which is too big. This might occur if the function is never going to stop because of a programming error, or if the argument is just too big.

>   OCaml

```
# let rec f x = 1 + f (x + 1);;
val f : int -> int = <fun>
# f 0;;
Stack overflow during evaluation (looping recursion?).
```

Find the cause of the unbounded recursion, and try again. If it is really not a mistake, rewrite the function to use an accumulating argument (and so, to be tail recursive).

Exception: Match_failure ...

This occurs when a pattern match cannot find anything to match against. You would have been warned about this possibility when the program was originally entered. For example, if the following function f were defined as

```
let f x = match x with 0 -> 1
```

then using the function with 1 as an argument would produce:

OCaml

```
# f 1;;
Exception: Match_failure ("//toplevel//", 1, 10).
```

In this example, the match failure occurred in the top level (i.e. the interactive OCaml we are using), at line one, character ten.

Exception: ...

This is printed if an un-handled exception reaches OCaml.

OCaml

```
# exception Exp of string;;
exception Exp of string
# raise (Exp "Failed");;
Exception: Exp "Failed".
```

This can occur for built-in exceptions like `Division_by_Zero` or `Not_found` or ones the user has defined like `Exp` above.

WARNINGS

Warnings do not stop an expression being accepted or evaluated. They are printed after an expression is accepted but before the expression is evaluated. Warnings are for occasions where OCaml is concerned you may have made a mistake, even though the expression is not actually malformed. You should check each new warning in a program carefully.

This pattern-matching is not exhaustive

This warning is printed when OCaml has determined that you have missed out one or more cases in a pattern match. This could result in a `Match_failure` exception being raised at run-time.

OCaml

```
# let f x = match x with 0 -> 1;;
Warning 8: this pattern-matching is not exhaustive.
Here is an example of a value that is not matched:
1
val f : int -> int = <fun>
```

Coping with Errors

Helpfully, it is able to generate an example of something the pattern match does not cover, so this should give you a hint about what has been missed out. You may ignore the warning if you are sure that, for other reasons, this case can never occur.

This match case is unused

This occurs when two parts of the pattern match cover the same case. In this situation, the second one could never be reached, so it is almost certain the programmer has made a mistake.

OCaml

```
# let f x = match x with _ -> 1 | 0 -> 0;;
Warning 11: this match case is unused.
val f : int -> int = <fun>
```

In this case, the first case matches everything, so the second cannot ever match.

This expression should have type unit

Sometimes when writing imperative programs, we ignore the result of some side-effect-producing function. However, this can indicate a mistake.

OCaml

```
# f 1; 2;;
Warning 10: this expression should have type unit.
- : int = 2
```

It is better to use the built-in `ignore` function in these cases, to avoid this warning:

OCaml

```
# ignore (f 1); 2;;
- : int = 2
```

The ignore function has type $\alpha \to$ **unit**. It has no side-effect.

Index

( ), xi
*, ix
**, xi
*., xi
+, ix
+., xi
-, ix
-., xi
/, ix
/., xi
::, x
:=, xi
=, ix
>, ix
&&, ix

accumulator, 2
append, x
array, xi
array, xi
ArrayLabels, 55

balanced tree, 85
begin, xi
binary search tree, 83
bit stream, 27
bitwise logical AND, 27
bool, ix
Buffer.t, 23
bytecode, xi
bytes, 24

CCITT, 39
channel, 21
char, ix
close path, 117
close_in, xi
close_out, xi
compression, 35

cons, x
constructor, x
conversion specification, 57

data
    compression, 35
    decompression, 35
decompression, 35
delaying evaluation, 11
dictionary order, 74
do, xi
done, xi

end, xi
End_of_file, 22
exception, x
exception, x

false, ix
fax
    compression, 39
    decompression, 39
fill path, 117
floating-point number, xi
flush output bit stream, 31
fold, 1
    over trees, 5
for, xi
forcing evaluation, 10
format string, 57
formatted printing, 57
fun, ix
function, ix

game tree, 93

hash
    function, 89
    table, 89

Hashtbl, 89
head, x
    function, 9

identity element, 2
if...**then**...**else**..., ix
in_channel, xi
include, 81
input channel, 21
input_char, xi
int, ix
interface, xi
interleave lazy lists, 12

labelled argument, 51
labelled modules, 55
labels
    partial application, 52
lazy list, 9
let, ix
let rec, ix
lexicographic order, 74
list, x
list, x
List.fold_left, 1
List.fold_right, 1
List.map
    with fold_right, 3
ListLabels, 55
log, xi
logical shift left, 28

match, x
max_float, xi
max_int, ix
min_float, xi
min_int, ix
module, xi
module, 81

More, xiii
`more-ocaml`, xiii
mutable record field, 18

name, ix
native code, xi
noughts and crosses, 93

`ocamlc`, xi
`ocamlopt`, xi
raise, x
OPAM, xiii
`open_in`, xi
`open_out`, xi
optional argument, 51, 53
 default value, 55
out_channel, xi
output channel, 21
`output_char`, xi

partial application, x
pattern, x, 63
pattern matching, x
PDF, 101
 array, 102
 coordinates, 118
 dictionary, 102
 graphics, 117
 indirect reference, 103
 name, 102
 operand, 117
 operator, 117
 stream, 103
 text, 123
 writing, 107
permutation, 71
polymorphic, x
`Printf.printf`, 57
`Printf.sprintf`, 57
punning, 52

raise, x
record, 15
 field, 15
Red-Black tree, 85
`ref`, xi
reference, xi
rewind function, 23

searching, 63
 in lists, 63
 in strings, 64
set, 79
 made from lists, 79
sig, 81
`sqrt`, xi
Standard Library, xi
standard output, 21

StdLabels, 55
string, ix
string, ix
StringLabels, 55
stroke path, 117
struct, 81

tail, x
tail function, 9
tail recursion, 73
TCP, 29
text
 line breaking, 126
 showing, 127
 splitting into lines, 123
tic-tac-toe, 93
trailer dictionary, 103
`true`, ix
try, x
tuple, ix
type, x
type, x
typesetting, 123

unit, xi
Util, xiii

while, xi
with, x

Printed in Great Britain
by Amazon